BRITISH TRADE POLICY IN ORISSA

ORISSA HISTORICAL SERIES NO. 4

BRITISH TRADE POLICY IN ORISSA (1803-1900)

BY

SUBASH CHANDRA BARIK

R. N. BHATTACHARYA
KOLKATA 2001

Publishers : **R. N. Bhattacharya**
Publishers and Booksellers (Exporters)
6, M. M. Feeder Road
P.O. Ariadaha, Kolkata - 700 057
Phone No : 564-7048, 91-33-5647048
E-mail No. rnbhatta@satyam.net.in

First edition : March, 2001

ISBN NO. : 81-87661-13-5

Price : **Rs. 500/-**

Printed at : **R. N. Bhattacharya**
6, M. M. Feeder Road
P. O. Ariadaha
Kolkata - 700 057

Dr. B. C. Ray, M. A. (Alld), Ph. D. (London)
Retired Professor and Head, Deptt. of History, Berhampur University, Berhampur
Visiting Professor of Harvard University (USA), Visiting Professor Jagiellonian University (Poland)
90, Budheswari Colony
Bhubaneswar - 6, Orissa

CERTIFICATE

*This is to certify that the work incorporated in this thesis is the bonafide research work carried out by **Sri Subash Chandra Barik,** Lecturer in History, V. N. College, Jajpur Road, under my supervision and guidance and the same has not been submitted previously for a degree.*

Dr. B. C. Ray

DECLARATION

The present study entitled "British Trade Policy in Orissa (1803-1900)" is based on original research work undertaken by me and no part of the thesis has so far been submitted for award of degree in Doctor of Philosophy by myself or by anybody to confer any degree or diploma from any University or Institution.

Place : Jajpur Road **SUBASH CHANDRA BARIK**
Date : 26.10.98

Dedicated in
Loving memories of
my parents

CONTENTS

ACKNOWLEDGEMENT

I feel highly elated to express my esteemed sense of gratitude and indebtedness to my revered guide Dr. B. C. Ray, M. A (Alld), Ph. D. (London), Retired Prof. and Head, Deptt. of History, Berhampur University, for suggesting this work and providing me necessary guidance through his active involvement at each and every step of this piece of work. Starting from the planning of the thesis to the completion of the manuscript. I will ever remember him not only for his prudent counsel, painstaking efforts, sustained interest, constant encouragement and constructive criticism throughout the course of the research but also for his amicability, joviality as well as fathomless love and affection for me. I am also grateful to his family members, specially Mrs. Labangalata Ray, for her co-operation and encouragement.

I wish to express my sense of gratitude to Major Sk. Mohiuddin, Reader-in-History, Paradeep College, Paradeep and Dr. Bhagaban Sahu, Lecturer-in-History, Aska Science College, Aska and Sri Ashirvad Mohapatra, Lecturer in Botany, V. N. College, Jajpur Road for their kind help, prudent suggestions, constructive counselling and encouragement during the course of the work.

My obligations to Dr. G. C. Mishra, Reader-in-English, V. N. College and Dr. Sandhyarani Das, Lecturer-in-English, V. N. College can never be thrown into oblivion for their moral support, constant inspiration and help during the entire period of the research work.

I express my heartful devotion and foremost indebtedness to my beloved elders whose blessings, inspiration, sacrifice and guidance are behind my success.

I am very much indebted to my wife, Minati Barik and my loving sister Seema for their genuine support, love, affection as well as inspiration and encouragement which paved my way for the smooth conduct of the research.

Expression and extension of thanks is too small an act to speak for the pleasant company and sincere co-operation of my friends and well-wishers, instead I would like to treasure those feelings in the depths of my heart.

I am very much thankful to the authorities of the Orissa State Archieves, Bhubaneswar, Parija Library, Utkal University, Bhubaneswar, Orissa State Library, Bhubaneswar, Board of Revenue, Orissa, Cuttack's Record Room and Library, National Archieves, New Delhi, National Library, Calcutta for giving me access to various source materials and documents.

Words run short to acknowledge my special thanks to K. J. Consultancy, 1, Dharmavihar, P. O. Khandagiri, Bhubaneswar (Phone - 471990) and M/s Tripathy Xerox, Cuttack for the neat and meticulous editing of the manuscript.

Above all, with a heart full of devotion, I bow my head to the Almighty, Lord Jagannath for fulfilling my aspiration of completing the work. I pray for His blessings to grant me quietude and tranquility.

It would also particularly like to thank my publisher R. N. Bhattacharya, Calcutta who took the initiative in publishing this book.

SUBASH CHANDRA BARIK

FOREWORD

Trade has been the key to economic prosperity of a country since the time immemorial. The traders in ancient period, contacted the other lands either for some earning for maintaining their livelihood or the adventurous ones went out to search for themselves some business for a better life in lands other than their own. It is noticed that marine trade through sea route, though hazardous was more profitable than the non-seaborne trade. Therefore, marine traders were mainly responsible for the rise of several ports on coastal belt. Evidences of the existence of several ports on coastal regions of India are available from the remnants of ruins or from references in the literary works or traditional accounts. In fact, there were several ports in ancient period on Coromandal coast, Malabar coast and Bay of Bengal. The local traders of merchantile community of India in their sailing boats could travel on high seas to distant lands such as Burma, Ceylon, Sumatra, Java, Borneo, China, Japan and also Arabian countries and their trading activities could be extended to the western world. The traders with their choice articles collected from domestic indegenous, manufacturing local industries could reach the distant lands in boats for sale of articles in overseas market and the rare attractive choice articles collected from the distant markets could be brought in return to the Indian ports for sale and such articles could pass to the interior rural sectors mainly through the river water connecting the ports, on coastal regions which were then the centres of high commercial activities. This helped the economic prosperity of the country.

When we come to later medieval period, we see, with the advent of highly enterprising, adventurous, trading companies of the seafaring European nations, such as Portuguese, Dutch, Danish and the French on the coastal belt of India, a new chapter in trade activities began to set in. The export of Indian goods from coastal areas and in turn import of choice commodities by the aggressive European traders, combined with better naval techniques armed with modernised military weapons could outbeat the Indian local merchants, with sailing boats in contrast to the more advanced engine-driven ships of the European world. As a result, the trade facilities in monopoly shape and the profits there of passed into the hands of European trading companies and that seriously affected the economic life of India.

It is the British East India company a leading European trading organisation, with inordinate ambition of acquiring wealth out of profit on trade appeared on coastal India. As their trade prospect at Balasore on the coast of Orissa was hampered, due to the silting of the river outlet, they shifted to Hooghly and from there, indulging in local politics, seized power of administration in Bengal. After being established in Bengal and mainly for establishing free communication and trade prospect felt the necessity of the conquest of Orissa to connect Calcutta with Madras and in 1803 Orissa came under the imperialist British regime from the hands of the Marathas. The trade oriented profit-motivated British administrative system in Orissa robbed the previous commercial benefits and capital formation ability to enrich themselves. As a result, the process of pauperisation was set in Orissa from which it was difficult for Orissa to escape.

It is the British trade oriented profiteering, exploitive British administrative system which made the ruled areas or the colonies poor and in general left them undeveloped or backward. On the otherhand, in return it made the British rich. It is needless to say that it was the trade which brought for them colonies and therefore, Britain emerged as a superpower of the world, so far imperialist hold over the colonies continued.

With the fall of imperialism and emergence and growth of new democratic and a few autocratic nation states, as it is found, trade has not lost its significance. It has received a new dimension, a phenomenon with renewed strength with the advance of science and technology. Trade is no longer confined to import and export of manufactured commodities for bare necessities of life. Many developed states, as a profession for earning foreign exchange indulge in exporting war materials and technology. The trade propensities of the multinations have utilised modern technological resources to spread their hands all over the world. It gives a new shape to trade activities in globalised form for better economic prosperity which has resulted in binding of almost all nations economically. The supremacy of multinations in the economic affairs worldwide, has as commented by some, has led to the rise of a neo-imperialism.

The trade-oriented economic life has been so shaped in the present world that, a strike of the multinations or a superpower rich country at some points in the globe rebounds in some sort of reaction in other parts of the world.

In this context the unique importance of marine trade and its impact in a different way on present life style, needs special attention as in the past, as stated above.

A lot of histories on political life has been written in India. Some economic histories have been attempted. But especially history of trade, either on marine or non-seaborne trade (trade through even land routes) has been very much neglected. Without the detailed study and research on trade a clear picture of socio-economic life of the colonial era will remain incomplete. If greater attention is paid by researchers and historians to this problem of history of trade, it would not only enrich the economic history of India but also throw new light reflected in a detailed picture of the transformation of social life of India. The work done by Dr. Subash Chandra Barik in this regard is a valuable contribution to the history of trade, a neglected area in historical studies. It is hoped it would inspire the young researchers and scholars to go ahead in this field of study to fulfil the lacunae so far not looked for.

Director
Centre for Advanced Studies in
History and Culture
Bhubaneswar-6

B. C. Ray

PREFACE

Trade is an important aspect of historical studies and is one of the less focussed aspect of Orissan history. Trade is one of the keys of the economic life in understanding the past. It is difficult to find out suitable starting and termination points in the economic history of a particular region within a particular period as history is a continuous flow of developments. The period from 1803-1900 is notable for the changes in the economic conditions of the people of Orissa with the establishment of British rule. In India, there was a lot of regional variations of economic structure, components and development process. In view of this, the present study titled **British Trade Policy in Orissa (1803-1900)** strives to undertake a study in the field of trade at regional level.

The main concern of this thesis includes analysis, growth and development of Orissa trade in 19th century. The period taken up for study begins with the British occupation of Orissa in 1803 and ends with the end of the century. It aims to examine the nature, impact of British trade, overseas trade, industries and import and export duties in detail.

Nineteenth century was a century of struggles, experiments and observations for the province. Orissa during this period contained the three modern districts

of Cuttack, Puri and Balasore. This period is most significant in the development of trade in Orissa. The impelling forces of Industrial revolution converted India as well as Orissa into a monopoly market for selling Britisher's machinemade finished goods and purchasing raw goods at a cheap rate. Due to the British monopolisation, the age-old flourishing cottage industries like Salt, Cotton and Metal which have been affording subsistence to many could come to a close. The Charter Act of 1833 brought about the end of the John Company's trade monopoly and introduced the free trade policy in Orissa. The Company's rule ended with the great Indian Revolt of 1857. Queen Victoria of England directly assumed the administration of India in 1858. But this abrupt transfer of power from company to crown did not change the nature and content of administration for better. The legacy of the old system continued till a culminating tragedy occurred.

The famine of 1866, the greatest catastrophe exposed the inherent defects of the British administration in Orissa. Steps were taken for the improvement of communications, trade, industry, export and imports. The Grand Trunk Road was completed in 1875. The railway lines were opened in 1897 connecting coastal regions of Orissa with Calcutta and Madras. In the year 1897, there was the retransfer of salt Agency of Orissa from Madras to British Raj. The development of roads, railways, canals and ports not only broke Orissa's isolation from the outside world but also facilitated export and import trade through mobility. As a result, the socio-economic cultural link of Orissa with other

parts of India began.

Little has been written on the British administration in Orissa during the period, much less on the problems of economic policy. Here attention is given to the conditions of the people and the process of economic changes due to the British trade policy in Orissa. For the sake of the detailed and dispassionate study of the different aspects of the British Trade Policy in Orissa (1803-1900), this work has been divided into seven chapters. Chapter I reflects the economic conditions of the people of Orissa with a background of the nature of the trade that prevailed before British conquest which includes communication, trade, industry and import and export policies. Chapter II, highlights the system of communication which is indispensable to understand the economic condition of a state. Roadways, waterways and finally railways, their conditions and developments are throughly examined. Chapter III contains a description of the inland trade during British rule, its decline and its economic impact on the people of Orissa. Chapter IV highlights on Orissa' s previous glorious maritime trade and its gradual decline by the British economic policies. Chapter V consists of two sections- Salt industries and Cottage industries. Industry played an important role in the economic prosperity of the people of Orissa. This chapter gives a graphic description of the process leading to the decline and destruction of the salt industry and the condition of cottage industries in Orissa which led to the growth of proverbial poverty and economic underdevelopment. Chapter VI examines with the import and export duties, reducing several overlapping and

confusing taxes imposed in the pre-British period by providing a uniform, simplified and modernised system of taxes. The last chapter presents the conclusion and a critical account of the growth of abject poverty among the people of Orissa inspite of a few welfare measures like initiative in modernising the communication system, uniform tax system, contact with manufactured goods by the influence of industrial revolution, development of trade, imports and exports, adopted by the Britishers most of their benefits.

This work is mainly based on original sources consulted at the Orissa State Archieves, Bhubaneswar ; West Bengal State Archieves, Calcutta; National Library, Calcutta ; Board of Revenue Library, Cuttack ; Parija Library, Utkal University, Vanivihar ; and National Archieves, New Delhi. In these places I had access to the various documents, letters, reports, periodicals,. An humble attempt has been made to present an accurate picture of the trade of Orissa and its impact on the people during the period from 1803 to 1900. I have also given attention to the economic policies introduced by the Britishers. The present work touches the most important aspects of economic life of the people of Orissa. The means of communication, trade policies, industrial policies, salt policy and import and export policies and their consequences are thoroughly examined and highlighted in this work.

Some works on different aspects of the administration of Orissa both under the East India company and under the crown have been done by different researchers. But no work specifically on trade during early British period has so far been attempted. I hope this work will fill up the vacum in the studies on economic history of British Orissa.

SUBASH CHANDRA BARIK

Chapter - 1

ECONOMIC LIFE IN PRE-BRITISH ORISSA

The wealth and opulence of Orissa coupled with its better trading facilities had attracted outsiders and converted Orissa into a battle ground. Internecine warfare and successive foreign invasions have had an adverse effect on the economic life of Orissa since 1568 when prince Bayazid, the Afghan general conquered Puri, Cuttack and Balasore.[1] The Afghans could not succeed in consolidating their hold over this province for a longer period due to the rapid growth of the Mughal empire. Orissa fell a prey to the expansionist zeal of Akbar and his general Mansingh conquered it in 1592. Then it was apportioned into five sarkars and included into the Subah of Bengal.[2] The sarkars were Jaleswar, Bhadrak, Cuttack, Kalinga Dandapat and Rajmahendri. After more than one and half a century of Mughal rule, Orissa came under the sway of the powerful Marathas in 1751. The Marathas too could not prolong their supremacy over this land in the teeth of an imperialist British East India company which conquered the province on 14th October, 1803 and since then Orissa remained under the control of Bengal Presidency governed by a commissioner. The political subjugation of Orissa by Afghans,

Mughals and Marathas through successive ages became a formidable barrier for the revival of trade in Orissa.

For administrative convenience, the Marathas divided Orissa into two distinct revenue division-Mughalbandi and Garhjat. Mughalbandi stretched along the sea coast of nearly 8,000 square miles and was kept under the direct management of the Marathas. The hilly region held by the feudal chieftains, who were allowed to rule on fixed paying a quit rent or tribute to the Maratha government were called Garhjat. Thus, on the eve of the British conquest, Orissa consisted of three coastal districts of Cuttack, Puri and Balasore known as Mughalbandi areas and seventeen tributary states on the Garhjat areas.[3] The geographical tract stretching along the sea coast over a surface of 8000 square miles was called Mughalbandi with a population of about 11,25,000. The hilly regions stretching towards central India formed the Tributary mahals covering an area of 16,307 miles and having a population of about 3,37,500[4].

Progress and prosperity of a state depends largely on the development of trade. Trade is the way of livelihood or an occupation adopted by an individual or a homogenous group engaged in such equivalent activities. It may be hereditary or acquired. Trade may include the process of earning one's livelihood by manufacture or small scale selling away of products. For the development of trade, certain factors are responsible. They are communication, internal trade, external trade, industries and import and export duties.

There was no want of communications-roadways and waterways for the purposes of travel and merchantile traffic in Orissa of the eighteenth century. The country was intersected by a number of roads. Cuttack being situated on the river Mahanadi and occupying a strategic point served the purpose of a connecting link between Bengal, Madras and Nagpur. The familiar road that connected Bengal with Cuttack ran through Medinapur, Jaleswar, Basta, Ramachandrapur, Balasore, Soro, Bhadrak, Dhamnagar, Burwa, Arakpur and Padmapur.[5] This was the only route generally used by the pilgrims of northern India when they came to visit Puri. The same route was used by Motte in his march to Sambalpur in 1766. Leckie also used this road when he was deputed by Lord Cornwallis to Nagpur court in 1790 alongwith George Forster.[6] There was a regular road from Cuttack to Nagpur which passed through Banki, Baideswar, Padmavati, Kantillo, Belpara, Barmul, Baud, Sonepur, Sarangagarh, Mohra, Ratanpur, Maro, Lanji and Tharse to Nagpur.[7] There were two other roads from Cuttack to Nagpur which were not frequently used by the people or by the government as these roads passed through dense forests. Bengal-Cuttack road passed to Madras through Puri and Ganjam. The road from Cuttack to Puri was the continuation of Bengal-Cuttack road that passed through Balianta, Balakati and Pipli.[8] The main rivers of Orissa Subarnarekha, Dhamra, Salandi, Baitarani, Brahmani, Mahanadi, Kathjori, Kushabhadra, Bhargavi and Daya were navigable for several months of the year. In the interior there was a considerable amount of traffic along the rivers during the rains.

But generally these roadways were unmetalled and waterways were not properly bridged and impassable during rains. In the eighteenth century the country was filled with vast jungles in which tigers, bears and other ferocious wild beasts including lions were found.[9] The roads were not free from the nuisance of robbers and thieves.[10] The roads were mere fair-weather cart tracts without proper bridges and proper ferry arrangements. Orissa had a very inadequate means of communication, not a single all weather road existed. Port facilities were either not fully developed or waning out.[11] The waterways were mostly seasonal and confined to monsoon months. Due to lack of bridges and metalled roads, the rulers, zamindars, etc. used palanquins, horses and elephants as means of conveyance. Common people depended to a large extent on bullock carts, bhara and pack bullocks for the purpose of communication. Thus, Orissa remained underdeveloped for a fairly long period owing to lack of improvement in communication which retarded the growth of trade in Orissa.

Fertility of soil, availability of sufficient water and rising of two or three crops in the same land every year helped in production of grains in very large quantity. This generated not only the export capability of surplus grains to fetch money or foreign exchange but also made rice available for the consumption of the common people as well as the rich at a very cheap rate.[12] Orissa with her surplus agricultural as well as industrial products carried out inter-provincial and foreign trade. Orissa during 18th century had extensive trade relationship with Bengal, Bihar, northern India, Gujarat, Surat, Dacca, Kerala and the places in the eastern coast viz. Narasapur, Vizagapatam, Masulipatam, Pulicat, Madras and Modapallam.[13] The principal articles of export from Orissa to different places were rice, gram, butter, sugar, textile goods, gingelly seed, salt, iron, stone plates, copper, turmeric, sandal wood, lac, etc.[14] Orissa imported mainly articles like tobacco, spices, lead, silver, vermillion, aluminium, brine stone, dried fish, salt petre and various articles of luxury.[15] Rice being profusely cultivated formed the major part of export not only to different parts of Orissa but also outside Orissa. Rice was exported to Bengal[16] and other foreign countries like Maldive islands. Balasore was the great rice exporting port from where the stored rice was sent to different parts of Bengal. Orissa had excellent and extensive cloth manufacturing areas.[17] The vitalisation of commercial activities became increasingly apparent with the coming of a host of European traders and the rise of merchant enterprenuers to Orissa. Towards the end of the 17th century, the adverse geographical forces and unfavourable political atmosphere under the Mughals and the shifting of the seat of the chief and council of the East India company from Balasore to Hooghly and the lack of adequate interest of the foreign merchants brought the decline of the coastal trade.[18] But due to the patronage of Marathas, there was a profitable brisk trade. Salt and cloth were important articles to be exported in plenty. Thus, with limited wants or requirements, availability of rice, the principal consumable commodity at a very cheap rate together with plenty of cereal, salt, oil and such other articles, exporting grains and other home-made industrial products to fetch money, the man of the age, lived as much in happiness as the people of other ages, past and present.[19]

Being situated on the shore of the Bay of Bengal and having enjoyed all the privileges to develop her maritime trade, Orissa from time immemorial had her reputation as a seafaring country. In the glorious ancient period the ships of Kalinga helped the people in establishing colonies in the Indian Archipelago.[20] It is said the people of Kalinga were the pioneers in colonising the far-off islands of Sumatra, Java, Indonesia, Burma, Siam, and other places.[21] The main ports of Orissa from which the Kalinga ships piled were Masuli Patnam, Kalinga Patnam, Chilka, Puri, Chitrotpala, Hijli, Tamralipti, Harishpur and Balasore. The maritime trade with Indian Archipelago, Burma and other islands brought a vast amount of wealth to Kalinga. The glories and prosperity of ancient Orissa was probably due to her foreign trade and commerce with the distant lands.[22] It is well-known fact that prior to the arrival of European traders, the Indian merchants with trade centres in Balasore and Pipli carried on extensive coast-wise trade with the Malaya-Indonesian Archipelago.[23] The lack of royal patronage, the indifference of the muslim power to the prosperity of some ports, away from the headquarters of the muslim governors and the control of some important ports and strategic coast areas by the muslim administrators exclusively for the aggrandisement of the Mughal empire presented a new atmosphere in the maritime activities of the country.[24] During the reign of the Mughals, Balasore, Pipli and Harishpur came to much more prominence as important trade and naval centres on the coast of Orissa.

With the coming of the European merchants and the establishment of European factories, Orissa's trade with many countries of Asia and Europe took a different dimension. Orissa's chief articles of export through the European merchants were cloth, sugar and iron, rice, butter, silk, salt petre, lac, turmeric, wax and opium. Cowries which were imported to Orissa from the Maldive islands were also exported from Orissa to Europe. The commodities imported into Orissa from Europe were broad cloth of various colours, scarlet, bullion of gold and silver, copper, lead, vermillion, coral, glasses, knives, brim stone spelter, ivory and some articles of luxury.[25] Under the patronage of Marathas salt and cloth were important articles to be exported in plenty. The ports of Harishpur, Pipli and Balasore prospered and became centres of commercial activities, full of din and bustles. Ship building centres were found at Balasore and ship building became a profitable trade patronised by Maratha government. Thus, trade of Orissa was beneficial and prosperous on the eve of the British conquest of Orissa.[26]

Although agriculture formed the main feature of the economic life of the people of Orissa, yet, there existed several crafts and industries involving the employment of a large number of artisans and craftsmen. As it seems, a considerable portion of Orissa's population earned their livelihood working as manufacturers of various kinds of agricultural and non-agricultural products. The abundance of the products was such that even after the full needs of the people were met, there was left considerable surplus for export. Production of manufactured goods by indigenous people for their local consumption was a long established tradition in Orissan economy and the people of medieval Orissa manifested their industrial genius by working in various industries such as textile, boat and ship building, jewellery and works in iron, different metals, woods, stones, ivory, shell pottery, sugar, salt, salt petre refining, oil, liquor, perfumery, lac, wax, honey, etc. The industrial activities of the people adequately catered to the needs of all sections of the society. Not only did the manufacturers supply the necessary as well as luxury articles for internal consumption but also their surplus products could be exported for high profits to distant foreign lands like England, France, Holland, Maldive islands, Mallaka, Nagapatam, etc. Being a self-sufficient country her import was less than her export. Industries were kept alive by traders both native and foreigners, as well as by the patronage of the government. The British, French and other foreign traders paid 'Dadni' (advance) to the workmen at their places as it was a universal system of booking one's requirements before hand and took delivery of the goods usually in time before the sailing of the ships abroad. The agents employed by the traders had to supervise the work of the workmen.[27] The industries kept many people employed and afforded a modest means of livelihood to several hundreds of the people of the country. Towards the close of the Mughal rule, the industries began to decline due to (1) Salt monopoly adopted by the English in Bengal, (2) Unfavourable political atmosphere under the Mughals and (3) Lack of adequate interest of the foreign merchants. But under the patronage of Marathas, industries prospered. The manufacturers of Orissa especially in muslin, cotton and silk textile had a wide range of demand in the asiatic markets. The merchants went to Bantom, Pegu, Tennaserim, Achim and even to the red sea's ports of Aden and Jeddah in middle-east.[28] The export of commodities of Orissa like sugar, textiles, muslin, earthen pots and other handicrafts was a net addition to the economy of this province. It reflected the industrial prosperity of Orissa before British conquest.[29]

Production of salt in Orissa had been referred by Mandelso in the thirties of the seventeenth century.[30] Thomas Bowery in the seventies of the 17th century referred to the manufacturer of salt in Orissa by the people living by the sea side. According to him many people also during the dry season of the year moved to the sea side to manufacture salt.[31] As known from the english factory records salt was exported from Orissa to Bengal and Patna in the fifties and sixties of the 17th century.[32] These details show that production of salt formed a part of economic life of some people in Orissa. In the pre-British days salt production in Orissa was in a flourishing stage and of great commercial importance because it had a reputation for its quality, cheapness and plentiful supply. The people knew well since time immemorial the art and skill of producing the finest salt of all India. During the rule of Muslims and Marathas, despite political problems, the industry was not much disturbed. Salt was not only exported to Calcutta but was sent by way of the grand trunk road along the Mahanadi to Sambalpur and Berar and likewise by that of the Bamanghati pass in Mayurbhanj more than three lakh mounds of salt were being exported annually.[33] After the occupation of Bengal, even the East India company was taking 68,269 mounds per annum from Orissa before they conquered it.[34]

A flourishing salt trade brought to the Maratha government and annual revenue which exceeded the amount of land revenue derived by them in this province. Towards the close of the 18th century, an economic struggle had developed on the issue of salt trade between the Maratha government in Orissa and the East India company in Bengal. In 1784 an order was passed and executed by the East India company in Bengal that no merchants except the company's would be allowed to import salt from Orissa under the Maratha government to Bengal.[35] Britishers thus excluded the merchant of Orissa in the salt trade. The problem continued till the British occupation of Orissa.[36] Thus, on the eve of the British conquest of Orissa salt manufacturing provided a means of livelihood to thousands of people of the coastal Orissa and there was a profitable brisk trade by traders which prospered the economic life of Orissa.

Import and export duties on various articles formed an important aspect in the field of trade and commerce. The people of Orissa, under the Mughals, were subjected to various kinds of taxes and duties. Eventhough the merchants paid the normal duties their commercial activities were not free from difficulties. To a great extent, the conduct of trade depended on the privileges secured through farmans, nishans, parwanas and dastaks granted by Mughal emperors, princes, subahdars and diwans respectively. The peasants' annual contribution towards the land revenue normally varied between Rs. 34,00,000/- to Rs. 56,00,000/- which constituted the major source of income of the imperial government from Orissa, Further, about Rs. 9,00,000/- per annum was collected as pilgrim tax from the people who visited Lord Jagannath of Puri.[37] Besides the levy of land revenue and custom duties the imperial government also imposed various 'abwabs' or illegal cesses in one pretext or other, on the different sections of the society. As a result of this imposition, the local zamindars, chiefs, the merchants and the cultivators had to suffer a lot. Offering "nazar" was a common practice at the time. The kings received nazar from the subahdars and the subahdars from the zamindars and the zamindars from the people. Succession fees to the maximum amount of Rs. 10,000/- was bound to have been collected from some of the feudatory chiefs. The traders and merchants were subjected to customs, octroi and transit duties. They also had to offer presents, bribes, etc. to the ruling authorities in lieu of certain trade privileges. As a result the burden of taxes, duties and presents, sometimes remained unbearable and cast heavily on the economic condition of the people.

During the Maratha rule the usual normal practice was to allow various allowances in money or land to the revenue officer together with other expenses of collection and authorised deductions in the expenses. There ramained surplus of about four lakhs to be annually despatched to the court of Nagpur.[38] Roads were a source of income to the state. Two types of taxes were collected on the way from the people coming from outside into Orissa. One was custom duty, the other was pilgrim tax.[39] "Rahdars" (collectors of tolls or transit duties), "Guzarbans" (officers appointed to take tolls both on high roads and ferries), "Mustafizans" (custom peons) were appointed on the roads and ferries for the purpose of collecting taxes.[40] It is only those who got dastak or free pass were exempted from paying the tax. A bullock load of silk was taxed at six rupees and so on in proportion to the bulk and value of load.[41] Twelve Chaukis were established between Rajghat and Balasore for collecting money from pilgrims going to the temple of Lord Jagannath.[42] But the source of revenue collection from excisable articles was negligible during the Maratha period.[43] Thus, Marathas' tax pattern was traditional, fitting to the growth or sustenance of community life.[44] and the economic life of Orissa under the Marathas was comparatively better.

Under the influence of Renaissance and the geographical discoveries of the 15th century the nation states of Europe were inspired by a new spirit of adventure in distant places. This brought the traders of Europe- the Portuguese, the Dutch, the English and the French, to establish their trading settlements in different parts of India. The Britishers had obtained certain concessions from the Mughal ruling authority at the centre and its governors in the subahs[45] to establish their settlements. Orissa's trade received great encouragement with the establishments of European factories. The coming of the English into Orissa as merchants and the establishment of trading settlements on the Orissa coast dates back to the fourth decade of the 17th century. The British merchants long before their appearance as rulers in the political horizon of Orissa established their commercial settlements at Hariharpur or Harishpur, the modern Jagatsinghpur district[46] and subsequently the English factories sprang up at Pipli in Balasore district and Balasore proper.[47] The European merchants controlled the whole of Orissa's external trade by establishing contact with the merchants of Orissa and with producer of different articles of investment. Amongst all the Europeans, the English had a better share in the external trade of Orissa. The two harbours of Orissa, Balasore and Pipli, formed the basis of future greatness of Bengal[48] and the prominence of Balasore as a commercial centre continued for a long time. It declined in the 18th century when the East India company's trading concerns were shifted to Hooghly and Calcutta.

The 18th century was the period of colonial development of the european powers all over the world. The industrial revolution in England, not only revolutionised the units of production but also necessitated to annex more territories. The East India company had been endeavouring to acquire Orissa to connect the two seats of their government at Madras and Calcutta since the days of Robert Clive in Bengal.[49] The British political supremacy in Bengal reacted on the economic condition of Orissa which under the Marathas deteriorated in comparison with the condition of the previous period. Previously a large amount of salt was sold at Calcutta and other parts of Bengal. But in consequence of the application of salt monopoly there, that remained unsold. Consequently the income of Orissa from sale of salt to Bengal came to a stop except through smuggling.[50] The British merchants discouraged the export of grain from Orissa either to Bengal or to Madras. Consequently, this export trade which previously fetched economic advantage deteriorated to a very considerable extent.[51] The European merchants had already occupied the principal ports on the Bay of Bengal. They now controlled the trade on the coasts. The Oriya merchants failed to compete with them. As a result the export trade of Orissa in all other articles as in grains deteriorated considerably.[52]

No other government perhaps could have done more good than that of the Marathas within so small a period of merely about 53 years particularly when they were successors to an administration which was then in a state of utter confusion and had to rule Orissa at a time when a imperialist power like the British with superior military resources and techniques was adopting from Bengal an adverse economic strategy to strangle or impoverish the neighbouring state of Orissa into submission or occupation. All facts stated above explain the deteriorating economic condition of Orissa, generally because of the appearance of the British in the neighbouring state with adverse non co-operative and damaging economic tactics for their own profits.

REFERENCES

1. H. M Elliot and J. Dowson, Tarikh-i-Daudi, Vol. IV, pp. 41-51.

2. Abul Fazl, Ain-i-Akbari, Translated by H. S. Jarrett, Vol. 11, p. 138.

3. Maddox Report, Vol. 1, p. 1.

4. Bengal revenue proceedings, March 18, 1815, No. 29, J. Richardson to Government, December 20, 1814.

5. J. Runnel, Memoir of a map of the Mughal empire, p. CXXX.

6. Early european travellers in Nagpur territories, p 52.

7. Ibid. p.52

8. J. Sarkar, History of Bengal (ed.), 1950 Vol. II, pp. 208-09.

9. Calender of Persian Correspondence, Vol. V, 1978.

10. B. C. Ray, New lights on Maratha Orissa, 1993, p. 187.

11. L.S.S.O.' Malley, Bihar and Orissa district gazetteers, Puri, 1929, pp. 212-213.

12. B. C. Ray, New lights on Maratha Orissa, 1993, pp. 225-226.

13. Imperial gazetteer of India, Provincial series, Madras, I, pp. 323-326.

14. Proceedings of Indian historical congress, 16th session, Waltair, 1953, p. 220. E. F. I. Vol. VI, 1637-1641.

15. Bengal, past and present, Vol. 79-80, Serials 147-148, 1968, O.H.R.J., Vol. VII, Part-3 & 4 1958-59, p. 208, p. 27.

16. Diaries of Streynsham master Vol. II and Hakluyt Vol. V, p. 409.
17. Proceedings, Indian historical records commission, Vol. XIV, 1937, p. 92.
18. B. C. Ray, New lights on Maratha Orissa, 1993, p. 227.
19. B. C. Ray, New lights on Maratha Orissa, BBSR, 1993, p. 231.
20. R. D. Banerjee, History of Orissa, 1930, Vol. I, p.94.
21. Ibid, p. 98, It throws some light as the people of Kalinga taking part in colonising these islands.
22. B. C. Ray, Orissa under the Mughals, 1981, p. 138, Proceedings of Indian history congress, 14th session, Jajpur, p. 172.
23. B. S. Das, Studies in the economic history of Orissa, 1978, p. 228.
24. L. N. Rout, Socio-economic life under the Muslim rule in Orissa, Punthi prakashan, 1988, p. 270.
25. J. N. Sarkar, Studies in Mughal India, 1950, p. 320.
26. B. C. Ray, New lights of Maratha Orissa, 1993, p. 226.
27. Ibid, p. 226.
28. Moreland, A study on the Indian economic history (Indian edition), 1972, pp.30-49.
29. Dairy of William Hedges, Vol. II, London, 1681-87, p. 239.
30. Johann Mandelso in John Harris, "A collection of voyages and travels, Vol. I, p. 780.

31. T. Bowery, A Geographical account of countries round the Bay of Bengal 1669 to 1679, p. 199.
32. European factories in India, 1655-1660, Vol.X, p. 297.
33. B. C. Ray, Foundations of British Orissa, 1993, p.205.
34. Ewer to Govt. on 13.5.1818, Revenue consultation, No. 15, July 17, 1818.
35. Calender of Persian correspondence, Vol. VI, No.1242.
36. B. C. Ray, Orissa under Marathas, 1978, p.83.
37. L. N. Rout, Socio-economic life under Muslim rule in Orissa, Punthi prakashana, 1988, p. 305.
38. B. C. Ray, New lights on Maratha Orissa, 1993, p. 10.
39. Ibid, p. 186-187.
40. Calendar of Persian correspondence, Vol. VI, No. 496, Vol. VII, No.232.
41. Early european travellers in Nagpur territories, p. 56.
42. B. C. Ray, New lights on Maratha Orissa, 1993, p. 187.
43. G. Toynbee, A Sketch history of Orissa, 1873, p. 66.
44. B. C. Ray, New lights on Maratha Orissa, 1993, Preface p. 1.
45. Kalikinker Dutta, Survey of India, Social life and economic condition in the 18th century (1707-1813), 1961, p.22.
46. Bengal District Gazetteer, Balasore, p. 37.
47. Ibid, p.33, W. W. Hunter, History of Orissa, Vol.

II, 1878, p. 39.

48. W. W. Hunter, History of Orissa, Vol. II, p.39.
49. B. C. Ray, Foundations of British Orissa, 1960, p.12.
50. 13 May 1818, Ewer to Government, Bengal revenue consultations, 17 July, 1818, No. 15.
51. Ibid.
52. B. C. Ray, New lights on Maratha Orissa, 1993, p.243.

Chapter - 2

MEANS OF COMMUNICATION

Communication is an important infrastructure and a catalytic agent for the rapid industrial and economic development of a state. If agriculture and industry are regarded as flesh and blood of the economy, communication is its nerve. In advanced countries, it is a means to social welfare. They spend more resources on communication development and transport innovation. For a developing country like India, which was underdeveloped during the British rule, communication was specially important to accelerate the process of economic development. It is to infuse economic mobility in the living pattern of Indians and specially at present for agrarian, industrial and technological development. A sound and effective transport network is considered as the primary requirement. If transport network is poor, incomplete, unreliable, costly and slow, it affects production activities, increases cost of production and pushes prices up often beyond the reach of the consumers. Hence, it would not be improper to consider communication as an industry and branch of material production.[1]

If India was economically poor, Orissa was poorer one, and her communication system was directly proportionate to her poverty. Orissa had a very inadequate means of communication during the 19th centrury. Railway facilities were limited, road facilities were inadequate and port facilities were either not fully developed or waning out.[2] Economy of Orissa remained underdeveloped for a fairly long period owing partly to the lack of improvement of communication.[3]

The communication which were developed in Orissa may be analysed under following heads.

Roadways

Orissa was connected with Bengal and Bihar by several roads during 18th century. Cuttack being situated in a strategic point, served the purpose of a connecting link between Bengal, Madras and Nagpur. It was the only town between Bengal and southern Sarkaras. The familiar road passed from Ganjam to Calcutta via Malud, Manikpatna, Cuttack, Jajpur, Bhadrak, Soro, Balasore, Jaleswar, Narengarh, Purtabpur and Budge Budge. The distance from one place to another has given below.

ROADS	DISTANCE IN MILES
01. Ganjam to Malud	17
02. Malud to Manikpatna	20
03. Manikpatna to Puri	20
04. Puri to Pipli	22
05. Pipli to Cuttack	26
06. Cuttack to Jajpur	41
07. Jajpur to Bhadrak	19
08. Bhadrak to Soro	19
09. Soro to Balasore	22
10. Balasore to Ramachandrapur	9
11. Ramachandrapur to Basta	9
12. Basta to Jaleswar	14

13.	Jaleswar to Narayangarh	25
14.	Narayangarh to Bancychak	10
15.	Bancychak to Purtapur	19
	TOTAL	***292***[4]

These were the routes generally used by pilgrims when they came to visit Puri.[5] The same route was used by Motte, an officer of Robert Clive in his march from Bengal to Sambalpur.[6] Lackie also used this road when he was deputed by Lord Cornwallis to Nagpur Court in 1790 A.D. along with George Forster.[7] Orissa was also connected with Madras by a road that connects the Ganjam Calcutta road beside the Chilka lake. Alexander Hamilton came from Madras to Ganjam through this road in 1708 A.D.[8] Orissa was connected with Golkonda (south) by a road through the Chhatar Diwar pass.[9] In the west also, Orissa was connected with Nagpur. The road from Cuttack to Nagpur was bifurcated at Sarangagarh one leading to Sambalpur and other to Cuttack through Sonepur. In 1743 A.D. Raghuji Bhonsle came to Cuttack through this road.[10] Khurda was not connected with Cuttack and Ganjam directly during the period of Maratha administration. Dense forest regions between Khurda and Ganjam did not permit the Maratha rulers to construct direct roads between Khurda and Ganjam. A road which connected Khurda with Puri passed through Sahajapur and Kalupada crossing Daya river and joined with the main Cuttack-Puri road at Pipli.[11] These important roads were used by the people for mercantile traffics.

Orissa remained undercivilised and underdeveloped for a fairly long period owing to lack of improvement in transport and communication. Orissa was geographically isolated from the outside world. Most parts of Orissa region remained remote and inaccessible and people lived in ignorance, superstition, caste prejudice, irrational customs and traditions. There were no other roads in the real sense and their absence made the province inaccessible. Buchman wrote, "There were no good roads in most parts and built earlier by earth works, were unsatisfactory and impassable during rainy season.[12] When the British took over the province in 1803 A.D., there was not a road in the modern sense of the word. What were then called roads were mere fair-weather cart-tracts without bridges and without proper ferry arrangements for crossing numorous water-courses which they intercepted. They passed through the most part over high ridges of uncultivated land.[13].

The traffic from south to Cuttack passed along the eastern coast of the Chilka lake and hence followed exactly the line of Jagannath Sadak, which was constructed in 1811-12 A.D. and completed in 1825 A.D. Another line from Puri passed through Khurda and Barmula pass into the central provinces via Sambalpur. The greater part of the earth work of the Jagannath Sadak between Cuttack and Puri was completed but it was not open to traffic till 1817 A.D.[14]. The grand trunk road which ran through the province afforded communication with Midnapur and Calcutta in the north and with Ganjam in the south.

It was built by captain Sackville between 1812-1820 A.D. The metalling of this road was not done properly. The floods and inundation played havoc in Orissa and wasted away many parts of the roads which needed repair and proper bridges.[15] This isolation and inaccessibility was many times aggravated by the ravages of famines in Orissa. It was also responsible for the decline of trade, commerce and manufacture of traditional items.[16] The Britishers realised the importance of transport and communication.

The grave deficiency of communications which still existed as late as 1866 A.D., was seriously exposed in the great Orissa famine. It was said that the people were shut between pathless jungles and impassable seas and were like passengers in a ship without provisions. The complete absence of the good means of transport was one of the principal causes of the famine of 1866 A.D. The famine commission of 1867 submitted a report that the whole province was geographically isolated to an excessive degree. To the north and north-east, the hill tracts are contiguous to countries more hilly, wild and inaccessible by which they were separated effectually from central and northern India. On the other side, the nature of the coast and the sea stopped all the native traffic for the major part of the year with an exception of the false point. There was no protected anchorage of any kind. Such being the difficulties on the either side of the length of Orissa, the only ordinary mode of communication with the outside world was by the route traversing its length. The wheeled carriage, pack bullocks were still, pre-dominant at all times. In rainy season, wheeled traffic was quite impracticable and when the rains were heavy even pack-bullocks were not used. The people carried their luggages on head and walked for miles together.[17]

The famine commission of 1867 A.D. strongly recommended the speedy improvements of roads, canals, ports and railways to provide easy and cheap communication to different parts of Orissa to break isolation and to bring the province in touch with outside world.[18]

After famine of 1866 A.D., government began to give attention to the construction of the new roads and maintenance of the old ones. The grand trunk road from Madras to Calcutta via. Orissa was completed by public works department in 1875 A.D. This road was one of the most important highways passing through Orissa. Its length was 338 miles. This trunk road entered into Cuttack district at Akhuapada, 46 miles from Cuttack city. It was a metalled road and people were crossing the rivers-Mahanadi, Baitarani, Brahmani and Kharsua by ferries. From Cuttack city a branch line was connected with main Calcutta highway road which was running from the south to the town of Puri. The total length of roads in Orissa upto 1877 A.D. was 531 miles.[19]

Roads were constructed and maintained by different agencies. Provincial roads were paid out of provincial funds and were kept under the charge of public works department of the provincial government. The second category of roads were paid out of the district road fund and were under the charge of the district engineer. The local board roads were maintained by the local boards for local utility. The cost of the maintenance of such roads were paid out the local funds.[20]

There were two provincial roads. The one Cuttack-Sonepur road was mostly unmetalled and the other, Cuttack-Sambalpur road was stretched upto the bank of the river Mahanadi. The principal district board roads were leading to Cuttack town. A good many roads were connected Cuttack with some other sub-roads. These were :

01. Cuttack to Taladanda-44 miles in length, out of which 14 miles were unmetalled.

02. Cuttack to Machagaon-32 miles leaving Taladanda road 11 miles metalled up to 14 miles from Cuttack.

03. Cuttack to Chandabali road passed through Pattamundai having a length of 63 miles.

04. Phulnakhara to Madhab road joined with the Cuttack-Puri road at 15 miles from Cuttack.

05. Tangi to Haripur road connected the Garjats with grand trunk road at 10 miles from Cuttack.

06. Jajpur to Kuakhia was a bad road with a length of 30 miles. It was not bridged at the river Kharsua and the Baitarani.

07. Jajpur to Kendrapara road connected these two important towns for commercial benefits with a length of 25 miles.

08. Beran to Kalamatia was inaccessible during rains and its length was 16 miles.

09. Jajpur was connected with Pachhikote estate by a road. This road was 19 miles long and partly bridged.

10. Salipur to Chhatia road crossed two rivers having the length of 18 miles It was inaccessible during rains.[21]

In addition to the above roads, there were some other minor roads which were reconstructed in 1873 A.D. These were as follows.[22]

	ROADS	MILES
01.	Cuttack-Aul road	57
02.	Cuttack-Sonepur road	140
03.	Fakirpada-Machagaon road	40
04.	Jajpur-Kerasingh road	10
05.	Indupur-Pattamundai road	11
06.	Indupur-Kendrapara road	8
07.	Jagatsinghpur-Kujanga	5
08.	Jagatsinghpur-Tirtol	8
09.	Berun to Balichandrapur	14

The opening of roads facilitated the merchants coming from Calcutta and Madras to trade in forest produce and rice respectively.[23] They also penetrated into Garhjat tracts when the government connected Sambalpur and Cuttack by a road in 1879 which passed through Angul. In 1879-80 the British Raj had also collected voluntary cess from the tribals to construct roads in Khandamahal.[24] In the Sambalpur district huge sums had been spent to improve Sambalpur-Binka road and to repair Sambalpur-Raipur road. This resulted in the rise of volume of import and export from Sambalpur.[25] After 1885, Bargarh road and Sonepur road were repaired and metalled to open the area to the traders.[26]

At the turn of the century, Orissa was no longer an isolated province. It possessed the following metalled roads to enable the people to possess the benefit of the modern civilization.

Metalled roads of Orissa were as follows

Grand Trunk road
Sambalpur-Cuttack road
Ganjam road

Keonjhar road
Machagoan road
Taladenda road
Chandabali road
Jajpur road
Sambalpur-Bolangir road
Sambalpur-Raipur road.[27]

The chief road of the division was the Orissa trunk road which afforded communication between Calcutta and Puri. The road was excellent throughout, but there were difficulties in crossings at the Subarnarekha, Burabalonga and Brahmani rivers. The river crossings were troublesome only in the rain and early in the cold weather due to the absence of bridges. Systematic efforts were made to plant trees along Orissa trunk road. The metalling of the entire road was completed by 1927. As the only road to Puri from northern India, this road exhibited a constant stream of passenger traffic. With the inauguration of steamer service between Cuttack and Calcutta in eighteen sixties, the trunk road lost its importance as a pilgrim route. In the last years of 19th century only a small number of pilgrims travelled it. With the opening of railways during the closing years of 19th century, scarcely a pilgrim was to be seen, except an occasional fakir measuring his length along the road upon his toilsome journey southwards.

The Cuttack-Puri road (50 miles) was also maintained by the public works department. It was an excellent road through out. But the river crossings were troublesome until December as there were no bridges. Other important roads maintained by the public works department were the Khurda-Pipli road ($13^3/4$ miles), Khurda-Patnaika road ($12^1/2$ miles), Vyas-

Sarovar-Jajpur road (15 miles) and the Cuttack-Chandabali road ($63^1/4$ miles).[28]

The Cuttack-Puri road, also known as Jagannath or Pilgrim road was fifty miles in length. Before the completion of the railways, these roads used to be thronged with a continuous stream of pilgrims on their way to Puri, but foot traffic had now declined considerably and cart traffic was also growing less. It was, however, one of the most perfect roads with an over-arching avenue of trees, which afforded grateful shade to the footsore pilgrim.

Perhaps the most important trade routes were Cuttack-Khurda road, Pipli-Khurda road, and Bhadrak-Chandabâli road. The surplus produce of rice of the districts of Cuttack, Puri and Balasore were sent for export through these roads.[29]

Floods and inundation played havoc and washed away many parts of roads which needed repairs. The government needed more money for repair and maintenance of roads in Orissa. For this government collected public works, public funds and road cesses from the people of Orissa to be invested for road construction and repairs. The following statement shows the rate of road cess collected from peasants of different income groups.

Road cess collected in Orissa

Agriculturists whose annual income between :

Rs. 100 to 500 to pay	Rs. 0-8-8
Rs. 500 to 1000 to pay	Rs. 1-8-0
Rs. 1000 to 2000 to pay	Rs. 2-4-0

Business whose imcome from :

Rs. 250 to Rs. 1000 per annum to pay Rs. 2-4-0 [30]

In 1874-75 A.D. Cuttack alone collected road cess as follows :

Road cess credit balance	Rs. 23,005/-
Road cess current year	Rs. 27,997/-
Ferry tolls	Rs. 3,737/-
Government in aid	Rs. 5,000/-
Miscellaneous	Rs. 921/-[31]
Total	Rs. 60,660/-

Expenditure in Cuttack district for the original new road construction is given below :

1. Road cess Tahasil expenditure	Rs. 4,089/-
2. Chandabali road (15 miles)	Rs. 6,136/-
3. Binjharpur to Indupur road	Rs. 1,490/-
4. Salipur to Mahanga road	Rs. 1,220/-
5. Kendrapara to Marsaghai road	Rs. 800/-
6. Chandabali road bridge construction	Rs. 3,300/-
7. Repairing	Rs.25,527/-
8. Provincial revenue expenditure	Rs. 4,447/-[32]
Grand Total	Rs.47,009/-

Balasore district board constructed 38 roads having the total length of 309 miles. Only 40 miles were unmetalled and 269 miles were metalled. It was impassable during rains. In north Balasore, the Karada-Baliapalla-Basta road, Kamrada-Jaleswar and single Nangeswora roads were unsafe for traffic due to high floods during rainy season. In south Balasore, the Panchapada- Haldiapada road, Balasore-Nilgiri road, Gopinathpur-Nilgiri road, Bhadrak-

Chandabali road were in good condition for the passengers and commercial traffic. The traffic was heavy in both Chandabali and Basudevpur-Chandabali road, rice was exported in large quantities and many consumption articles were imported from Chandabali port. In addition to the district board roads, there were 67 village roads with a total length of 200 miles. These were all fair-weather roads.[33]

Road cess collected from the district of Balasore is given below :

The total receipts of the board amounted to Rs. 70,986.00. Out of this amount Rs. 17,670/- was spent on original works, Rs. 20,034/- on repairs, Rs. 5439/- on establishment and other miscellaneous heads leaving balance of Rs. 27,843/-. The board expended Rs. 2830-14-7 for the improvement of 67 village roads in 1888-89.[34]

The district board of Puri constructed the following old roads in the year 1885-86. These roads were :

01.	Pipli-Khurda road	14 miles
02.	Khurda-Kalapathar	18 miles (First 10 miles metalled)
03.	Baghamari and Balugaon	18 miles (katcha)
04.	Balugaon and Baghamari via Banpur, branches off from Ganjam trunk road.	72 miles (Open for traffic 15 miles)
05.	Barighai and Madhub	18 miles (katcha)
06.	Satyabadi and Jaipur	1 mile
07.	Astaranga road	2 miles
08.	Pattanaik-Khurda road	22 miles
09.	Puri-Babakudi road	4 miles
10.	Chandka to Bhubaneswar	10 miles [35]

The proposal and outlay on works during 1885-86 were as follows :

	Proposed	***Actual***
Original works	Rs. 18,037	Rs. 17,038
Repairs	Rs. 13,941	Rs. 8,665
	Rs. 31,978	Rs. 25,703

The grant for village roads in Puri was Rs. 65,146 in 1884-85 against Rs. 3,880/- in 1883-84. The expenditure amounted to Rs. 1,208/- against Rs. 1,223/- in 1884-85.[36] The district of Puri is traversed by two provincial roads which were in charge of the public works department. The Jagannath road from Cuttack to Puri was 53 miles out of only 10 miles was metalled. The most important district board roads like Pipli-Khurda 18 miles (metalled), Khurda-Kalapathar road 22 miles metalled and Khurda-Pattanaik road were completed metalled road at the cost of Rs. 10,500/-[37]. Besides three metalled roads, a portion of less important roads, the total length of 133 miles metalled repaired by the board at the cost of Rs. 15,420.[38]

In 1888-89, some new village roads were constructed & all existing roads, bridges, culverts and bungalows repaired in Cuttack district by the board. There were four new works taken in hand in Jajpur sub-division. These were Baliapalla road, Barachana-Balichandrapur road and Balarampur to Brahmani embankment. A new bridge was built over the right side of the trunk road. The total receipts of the district board in 1888-89 Rs. 1,14,450-6-3. of this sum Rs. 8249-4-1 was spent on original works, Rs. 39077-11-5 on repairs, Rs. 37420-12-0 on education.[39] In

Puri twelve roads under the district board were repaired at the cost of Rs. 20,000 in 1888-89.

The principal highway viz., the Cuttack-Chandabali and Cuttack-Taladanda canal roads opened for public traffic in 1888-89. The high level canal and the Kendrapara canal roads used as the means of communication between Cuttack and Bhadrak and Cuttack and Chandabali respectively. The following amounts were expended by the public works department in 1889-90.[40]

Original work	Rs. 4094-12-1
Repairs	Rs. 39929-15-3
Establishment	Rs. 4983-0-2
Total	Rs. 49012-11-6

The district board of Balasore maintained altogether 34 district roads. The Balasore-Malakula road was completed in 1889-90 at a cost of Rs. 7989. The total length of the district road was about 296 miles out of which 39 miles were metalled and 257 miles were unmetalled. In addition to these districts roads, there were 67 village roads with a total length of 200 miles under the control of Balasore sadar and Bhadrak road board.[41]

In 1894-95 A.D. the Cuttack municipality maintained a total length of 24 miles of metal road and 67 miles unmetalled road in the jurisdiction of municipality. The Balasore municipality maintained a length of 19 miles of metalled roads and 8.75 miles of unmetalled roads. The Puri municipality looked after 4 miles of metalled roads and 13 miles of unmetalled roads at the cost of municipality resources.[42]

In July 1894-95, there was heavy flood in the river Brahmani and Kharsua. The Brahmani river on the south and the Bura and Kharsua on the north were under water and all communications by the trunk road were stopped for a couple of days. The road from Cuttack to Jajpur having a length of 36 miles was submerged under some ten to fifteen feet of water. The four bridges and the metalled road of this line were washed away. The damages were soon repaired by public works department. The total outlay on original and repair works in 1894-95 amounted to Rs. 11,782 and Rs. 80,743 respectively. The district board of Cuttack spent Rs. 3,820 on a new road and the Kendrapara local board spent, Rs. 2,664 on five village roads. One masonary bridge and three culverts were constructed by the Balasore district board. A sum of Rs. 15,520 was spent on repairs of metalled and unmetalled roads and the sum of Rs. 5,294 in maintaining village roads.[43]

The following table shows the length of metalled and unmetalled roads maintained by the district board and local boards of Cuttack, Puri and Balasore districts during 1894-95.

Roads	***Cuttack District Board***				***Balasore District Board***				***Puri District Board***			
	District Board Miles	Local Board Miles	Munici-pality Road Miles	Total Miles	District Board Miles	Local Board Miles	Munici-pality Road Miles	Total Miles	District Board Miles	Local Board Miles	Munici-pality Road Miles	Total Miles
1	2	3	4	5	6	7	8	9	10	11	12	13
Metalled Road	26	-	24	50	44.25	-	19.0	63.25	75	-	4	79
Unmetalled Road	439	351	67	857	260.75	184.75	8.75	454.25	71	-	13	84

Source : AGAR of Orissa division 1894-95, Mr. H.G. Cooke, C.S.I, Commissioner of Orissa division No. 1059, Revenue dated 05.07.1895, Para-291

Towards the close of the 19th century, the roads of Cuttack, Puri and Balasore districts were given below :

	Metalled	Unmetalled	Total miles
Cuttack	57	925	982
Puri	83	117.25	200.25
Balasore	64.25	463.75	528

In 1898-99, Cuttack district spent a sum of Rs. 4,415/- on new road construction and Rs. 22829 on the repairs of district roads. The local board spent Rs. 5,863 on fifteen new village roads and Rs. 8,614 on repairs of 231 existing village roads. Puri district board spent Rs. 12,041 on new works and Rs. 12,538 on repair works. The important construction and repair work of the road was postponed due to famine relief work.[44]

For the purpose of inland communication, elephants were harnessed. Bullocks, buffalows and asses were also used. But the carts driven by the bullocks were very common and mostly used as the means of communication. Packhorses were used extensively for going to distant places whereas bullocks were used as means of transport.

Development of communication was the immediate necessity to protect the country from frequent occurrence of famines and scarcities. Britishers became interested in the development of these roads for the purpose of commercial prosperity. But the real attention of the government to road construction and repair was given after the great famine of 1866 and the development of road communication changed the nature of agricultural production from food crops to commercial crops. It provided the facilities for easy transportation of commodities from one place to another which helps to change the life style of the people of Orissa.

Railways

On 20 April 1853 A.D. Dalhousie issued his great railway minute describing the military and commercial advantages of railways recommending extensive project undertakings. For the military movements and to bring the bulk of the military strength, railways were necessary. From the commercial point of view, Dalhousie pointed out the England was calling aloud for the cotton which India produced and was expected to be sent from the distant plains to the several ports for its shipment by the proper means of conveyance. The board of control Sir Charles Wood supported Dalhousie's programme. The bigger railway undertaking began to take shape. The first railway line extending over a length of 34 km. from Bombay to Thana was opened for public traffic on 16 April 1853 A.D. The east Indian Railway from Howrah to Hooghly, a distance of 37 km. was opened for public traffic on 15 August 1854 A.D.[45] From 1853-54 A.D. India's railway system expended rapidly to become by 1910 A.D. the fourth largest in the world.[46]

In 1866, Orissa was visited by a famine of most intense and desolating character. Its severity was so terrible that about one third of the population died. Transport and efficient means of communication were regarded as the basic necessities for prevention of famines. In Orissa, these methods were adopted in haste and hence proved fruitful. The old means of communication through canals, rivers and muddy roads were given paramount importance in Orissa. The impact of western civilisation and fruits of industrial revolution such as railways and modern science did not reach at the people of Orissa compared to other states of India.[47] The Government of Bengal was not in favour to constructing railways in Orissa.

Appeals by the people for railways in 1878 was turned down by Lt. Governor with the plea of costly ventures (20 lakhs of rupees). He pleaded that heavy bridge works would involve huge cost; and hence, railways were not possible in Orissa. The utkal sabha under the leadership of Late. M.S. Das and Late. G. S. Roy, Editor of Utkal Dipika, mobilised public opinion in favour of construction of railway lines in Orissa[48]

It had been decided during 1870's not to proceed with railways in Orissa. The commissioner of the division, T.E. Ravenshaw was more inclined towards canals than the railways. In his opinion canals were more suited to Orissa than the railways.[49]

The Bengal government was also not in favour of the construction of the railways. It was believed that, heavy bridge works would involve huge cost and railways would not be remunerative. There was another reason too. After having spent much in the Orissa canals, the government was not prepared to incure huge additional expenditure on railways. The Lieutenant Governor Sir Richard Temple during his visit to Orissa in 1874 had been appealed by the people for the construction of railways but in vain.[50] A similar appeal had been made to Sir Ashley Eden, the Lieutenant Governor in March 1878 during his visit to the province. But Sir Eden considered it more worthwhile to proceed with cannals than railways in Orissa.[51]

It would have been better had the government decided to push further the original schemes of canals like the Pattamundai and high level canals, which would have connected in Calcutta with Puri along the important places of Orissa. This was in fact pressed for by the commissioner T. E. Ravenshaw in 1878. Sir Ashley Eden on the otherhand, planned for the coast canal which was a mistake. This canal, it was thought, would cost only Rs. 36 lakhs and it would protect the country against famine, while the railways would cost not less than Rs. 20 crores owing to the necessity of heavy bridging.[52] Sir Eden was a great champion of the railways and the development of railways in Bengal during his administration was very rapid.[53] Yet the proposal for Orissa was not acceptable to him.

When it was decided to construct railways in Orissa the coast canal had hardly been put to use. Lands were acquired and the construction commenced in 1895. While the work was in progress, A. Smith, the commissioner of Orissa, gave a proposal to connect Cuttack-Sambalpur by a branch line and to extend it upto Bilaspur with a view to monopolising the trade carried through Baramula. He hoped that it would connect coastal belt with Garhjat, a tract which was yet to be opened by the trunk road and canals.[54]

The Cuttack-Calcutta extension of the Bengal-Nagpur railway and a part of the east coast railway worked by the Bengal-Nagpur company, which passed through the three districts of Orissa were opened for through communication in 1899.

The Bengal-Nagpur railways was completed in 1898 and it was extended upto Sambalpur resulting in heavy export of rice and rise of the price of essential agricultural commodities.[55]

The works of east coast railways were carried on day and night to connect Calcutta with Madras via. Cuttack. It was finally completed and opened for traffic in 1895.[56] The opening of railway greatly facilitated the trade in rice and salt between Orissa and Madras.[57] During the turn of the century there was a demand for construction of a light railway line between Cuttack and Sambalpur. But it did not get a favourable wind.[58] A branch line to Puri was completed and opened for traffic in 1897. At the end of 1904 a light 2'-6" gauge railway connecting Baripada, the principal town of the tributary state of Mayurbhanj with Rupsa station of the Bengal-Nagpur railway was opened. It had been constructed entirely by the chief of the state, though for him by the Bengal-Nagpur railway company.[59] However, the railway transport facilities in Orissa were inadequate. The total length of railway constituted only 3 percent of that in the country (The Howrah-Madras and Howrah-Bombay, lines are passing through the eastern and the western parts of the state respectively. These lines which are touching the geographical boundary of the state). The length of that railway lines in Orissa are given below.[60]

	Total railway lines in Orissa	***Total railway lines in India***
Year	***Route in mileage***	***Route in mileage***
1899-1900	230	23,628
1930-1931	836	40,223
1936-1937	-	41,068

Orissa had only 7.5 miles of railway line per 100 sq. miles as compared to 11.2 miles in all India level, 19 miles in West Bengal and 25 miles in Bihar.

Commenting upon the harmful effect of railways in Orissa, economist G. V. Joshi remarked that the railways had the effect of "stamping out" the indigenous industries in an astonishingly short space of time and drawing the nation down to a fatal inclined plane to the verge of bankruptcy and ruin.[61] In the works of G. S. Lyre, "every additional mile of railway constructed in the country drove a fresh nail into the coffin of one industry or another".[62] The most detrimental effect of the railway policy was the constant draining of the raw materials of India. The growth of railways in India caused the destruction of vocations and occupations in a bid to economise labour by importing machines from abroad. The extension of railways promoted the interests of British trade and industry while it accelerated the decline of indian internal trade, cottage industries and handicrafts. They were fully exposed to competition from British manufactured goods as interior areas were opened up by railways. It also externalised the internal trade by moving goods from the interior to the ports at the expense of intra-regional trade. By facilitating the import of wheat and rice, even in famine years, it aggravated rather than mitigated the famines during the later part of the 19th century.

Despite this drawbacks, the opening of the railways marked a great change in the economic history of Orissa due to brisk trade of rice with different parts of India. The railways offered substantial advantage over more traditional modes of transport such as pack-bullocks, bullock-carts, camels, boats and human carriers. Railways helped indian agricultural commodities to become competitive internationally and made possible an enormous expansion in the export of products such as wheat, rice, jute, leather, oil-seeds and cotton. Agriculture began to commercialise. In the limited economic development, Orissa experienced that railways unquestionably played a major role. Railways led to increase agricultural output, the growth of modern industry and mining, new jobs, although many jobs were lost, the redistribution of the urban population, higher income for some segments of the population and numerous other economic changes.

Waterways

Besides the roads and railways, the principal rivers of Orissa were used as arteries of communication. The rivers like, the Mahanadi, the Brahmani, the Baitarani and the Burabalanga formed the great highway between the British districts of Orissa and the princely states of Orissa.[63] All these rivers were navigable. When the roads of Orissa were impassable for wheel traffic being muddy and unbridged, these rivers supplied an easy means of communication during the rain. River Mahanadi was the chief water route between Cuttack and Sambalpur through the princely states of Orissa like Athgarh, Athmallik, Banki, Baramba, Boud, Daspalla, Khandapara and Narasinghpur.[64] It provided the broad water-ways for the people of Talcher and Dhenkanal for nearly 8 months in a year. River Baitarani was of great use for the people of Keonjhar and Jajpur. In dry season also it was navigable as far as Anandapur. Navigation through these rivers were conducted by country boats and rafts. Transportation through these water routes was extensive because it was less expensive and there was no fear of way-side robbers and wild animals as in land routes.[65] Therefore a considerable trade was carried on through these rivers.

Ports

Being situated on the shore of the Bay of Bengal, Orissa, has retained its distinct identity as a great maritime power since the ancient times. It has not only enjoyed an extensive maritime trade with south-east asian countries but also had colonial settlements in southern Burma and Indonesian islands in ancient period.

The "Arya Manjusri Mulakalpa" a text of Mahayana Buddhism refers to all islands in the Kalinga sea as "Kalinga Dress". It seems that, the eastern sea or modern Bay of Bengal was known as "Kalinga Sagar" in the past because of its dominance by the ships of Kalinga. Kalidas, the celebrated poet of the 5th century A.D., in his Raghavamsa described the king of Kalinga as the Mahadadhipati, which means the Lord of the Ocean.[66]

Recorded evidences show that, there were four ports in ancient Orissa i.e. Tamralipti, Cha-li-ta-lo, Paluru and Pithunda. But these ports of Orissa lost their former glory and do not appear in the sources of modern Orissa. However, the British records reveal that modern Orissa possessed a number of ports like (1) False-Point, (2) Balasore, (3) Dhamrash, (4) Chandabali, (5) Subarnarekha, (6) Sartha, (7) Puri, (8) Ganjam, (9) Gapalpur, (10) Sunnapur.

Till the great Orissa famine broke out, in 1866, there were no ports of any significance in Orissa. All the ports that were there, were of little use when exposed to the ordeal of bad weather or any emergency. Hence, Orissa was generally inaccessible to the ordinary course of trade and was often found to have been cut off from the outside world. The famine commission recommended for the opening of some new ports and the improvement of the old ports. It gave a favourable response for the opening of ports to stimulate trade and to improve passanger traffic.

The Port of False-point

False-point, the most important of the ports in Orissa was situated at the mouth of the river Mahanadi. It was the best harbour on the whole coast of India between Hooghly and Bombay.[67] It was opened for traffic in 1860. But there was no means of good communication between the port and the interior of the country. After the famine of 1866 more attention was paid for improving this harbour. The harbour was surveyed and depended and the channels were buoyed. The work on the Kendrapara canal was speeded upto reach the tidal waters in direct communication with false-point. An agency had been established for the export of the commodities. The British Raj gave much importance to false-point port for its advantageous location and constructed buildings for office and godown to make it a modern port where goods got easy carriage to Cuttack through Kendrapara canal. In 1878, the government further sanctioned money for construction of a light house.[68] The light house was completed in 1880 and was able to cover a distance of twenty miles in the sea ensuring safety to the ships.

Balasore

Balasore port, which was situated on the south of river Burabalanga was a flourishing port because of its salt trade with Bengal and Madras. But the business of this port was declined in the second half of the 19th century due to sitting at the mouth of river Burabalanga. A large sum was required to revitalise the Balasore port. So the government, in order to avoid the huge expense, declared, Dhamrash as a port in 1858.[69]

Dhamrash

Dhamrash port was situated on the estuary formed by two rivers Brahmani and Baitarani. The port was opened for traffic in 1858, but was improved soon after the famine of 1886.

Chandabali

The port of Chandabali was situated on the mouth of river Baitarani. In 1867, it was declared as a port and named after T. E. Ravenshaw, the then commissioner of Orissa.[70]

Subarnarekha

Subarnarekha port, which was situated at the mouth of river Brahmani and Baitarani was also another seat of trade and commerce. But the dense jungles on the bank of the river afforded great opportunities for smuggling which was found difficult to check without expensive establishment.[71]

Puri

The only port of importance in Puri district was Puri. With the development of Chandabali and Puri ports, passengers began to go to Calcutta by steamer. [72] They also carried coconuts, oil seeds and rice from these ports. The ports of Puri drew the attention of the British government after the famine. They were Puri, Devee, Sahandu, Mettacooch, Futty pore and Nundla. There ports were in better position during the period under study but due to lack of proper supervision and maintenance they were turned to be roadstead. During the north-west monsoon, these ports did not allow vessels.[73]

Ganjam

Ganjam was an important port of the British period. It was situated on the mouth of river Rushikulya. It was developed as a port soon after the British established their factory at Ganjam in 1847-48.

About the port of Ganjam, T. J. Maltby in 1882 writes : "Once this was the chief port of the district, now it is a rere thing for a ship to come there."[74] This shows that, the ports of Orissa have lost their importance after 1880.

Gopalpur

Gopalpur (formerly known as Mansurkota) was the chief port of Ganjam district. It was situated at a distance of 9 miles from Berhampur. The depth of water in the encourage varied from 1/2 to 9 1/2 fathoms at low water. There were several bunglows at Gopalpur belonging to european merchants. F. V. J. Minchin the proprietor of Aska Sugar factory had an extensive godown at Gopalpur. The major maritime trade of south Orissa was handled by the Gopalpur port.[75] Large quantities of Sal wood sleepers were exported from Gopalpur to Madras and Calcutta for railway works.

Sunnapur

The port of Sunnapur was situated at a distance of 14 miles from Berhampur where river Bahuda falls into the sea. It was a minor port although in 1768 it was the principal shipping place in Ichhapur province.

Boats and rafts were used as means of transport. The boats described by T. Motte were very light, the plane being an inch thick and timbers small in proportion carrying from 600 to 700 maunds. And the largest he saw was 40 feet long and 4 feet wide.[76] Hunter has described all such boats as flatbottomed of about 25 tons of burden.[77] The palanquine was carried by four to six persons.

However, the ports of Orissa continued to decline after the 90's of the 19th century. There were several reasons behind this decline. Firstly the ports of Orissa fell into disuse by the deposit of mud and silt. The tendency of the Orissa rivers to silt at the mouths had been the main hindrances to the stability of every port. Secondly, the extension of railway system through Orissa during the 1890's accelerated the process of decline of the ports. Above all, the danger of pirates and hidden rocks posed serious problems to the seaborne commerce. Inspite of that, it can be said that, Orissa's trade was largely confined to coastal trade.

The importance of communication as a means of development of agriculture, industry and mining was less understood in Orissa during first half of the 19th century. The economy of Orissa remained underdeveloped for a fairly long period owing to lack of improvement in communication. Orissa was geographically isolated and the state was not in touch with the outside world. Most of the regions of Orissa remained remote and inaccessible and the people lived in ignorance, superstition, caste prejudice, irrational customs and traditions. This isolation of the province and inaccessibility to areas were the root causes for the aggravation of famines in Orissa. This was also responsible for the decline of trade, commerce and manufacture of traditional items. The successive famine commissions also recommended speedy improvements in roads, canals, and ports to provide easy and cheap transportation to different parts of Orissa to break isolation and to bring the province in touch with the outside world. Thus transportation for expansion of market economy and for stimulating internal and external trade, was highlighted after the famine of 1866. However, the famine broke the isolation of Orissa and improvement in transport was given paramount importance. Export and import got impetus. Cuttack was about 12 hours journey from Calcutta. Thus roads, railways and navigable canals constructed in the later part of the 19th century provided a link between Orissa and the outside world. This development also helped for the marked expansion of trade in the country.[78]

The development of roads, railways, navigable canals and ports not only broke Orissa's isolation from the outside world but also facilitated export and import trade by providing mobility to the people to move to different places in search of employment and reduced the liability of the province to famines. As a result, the socio-economic cultural link of Orissa with other parts of India began.

Communication broke the social barriers of religion, custom, untouchability and superstitution and brought together different people physically, socially and culturally. It enabled the people to travel to different regions. Customs, manners, languages and social contacts on a mass scale, enabled exchange of ideas, culture and knowledge. Social intercourse promoted culture and intelligence as well as understanding and outlook. In Orissa the development of postal facilities, mobile hospitals, and banks in countryside had been feasible, merely due to extension of communication facilities.

The greatest demerit of improved means of communication system was that it caused decline of the salt and weaving industries of Orissa as the foreign goods could be sold in the nook and corner of Orissa. Further, the increased exportation of rice due to this factor resulted in rise of the price of foodgrains. Gopabandhu Das rightly said, "Another point which I would urge in this connection and in which I have the strongest support of many people is the control of food stuffs and the restrictions on exports. The main difficulty in this way of leaving trade unrestricted lies in the varying economic conditions of different tracts. The workers in mills, for instance, can afford to pay for higher prices than ill-paid labourers in the more backward tracts and of the exports are unrestricted, the latter tracts might be denuded of their reserves of food which it would be difficult if not impossible to replace later on.

The development of communication was not upto the mark in Orissa during the 19th century. Several factors hindered the growth of means of communication firstly the government was callous towards the welfare of the people. Sums allocated for the development of communication was much less than what was necessary. Secondly, zamindars were apathetic towards the wants of the people although they got richer under the British rule. Thirdly, the local bodies did not carry out necessary welfare schemes because of the hidrances like internal dissersion, party feuds and paucity of funds. Fourthly, natural factors proved to be formidable obstacles in developing railways. Numerous rivers were flowing through Orissa. A large portion of Orissa was covered by hills, forests and sands.

Thus, it can be said without shadow of doubt that communication marked a great change in the trade of Orissa. The period on the whole was marked by impressive increase in trade. But the prediction that the development of communications would effects a complete revolution in the province, changing a backward isolated and unimportant country into a busy and prosperous centre of trade, however, did not prove true. The effects of this brisk trade, were not what had been expected. There was no increased wealth and comfort it was because of the fact that the trade of the province consisted in the export of food grains and other raw produce and import of finished goods. The improvement of communication gave the province the advantage of security against another famine by facilitating mobility of labour and importation of foodgrains.

REFERENCES

1. R. Agarkar, Regional Transport Development, Printwell Publishers, Jaipur (1989), p.1.
2. I. S.S.O.' Malley, Bihar and Orissa District Gazetteers, Puri (1929), pp.212-213.
3. Report of the commissioner appointed to inquire into famine in Bengal and Orissa (1866), Vol. I, p.5.
4. Renell, A Description of roads in Bengal and Bihar, pp.29-31. Journal of Asiatic Society of Bengal (1920-1924), p.107.
5. Sri Chaitanya Charitamrita, 1198, 112A (Sri Chaitanya went to Jajpur through Remuna).
6. T. Motte, "Journey to Sambalpur", OHRJ, Vol.I, Appendix-II, pp.1-49.
7. Ibid.
8. Alexander Hamilton I, A new account of the East Indies (1628-1723) pp.208-209.
9. R. D. Banerjee, History of Orissa from the earlier times to the British period, 1930, Vol.II, p.38.
10. Thornton Gazetteer, Vol.II, p.164.
11. J Sarkar, Studies in Aurangzeb's, Reign, 1950, p.230.
12. Francis Buchanan, "Economic condition in south and north India" (1880-1915), Quoted from H. K. Mishra's "Famine and Poverty in Orissa in 19th century", pp. 312-315.
13. S. L. Maddox, Final report on the Survey and settlement of the province of Orissa, 1890 to 1900 A.D. Vol. I, p.7.
14. Maddox Report Vol. I, p.8.
15. N. Senapati and D. C. Kuanr (ed), Orissa District Gazetteers, Puri (1977), p.275.
16. Indian Famine Commission, 1880, Part-I, p. 43, also see W. W. Hunter, Statistical account of Bengal, Vol.XVII and XIX.

17. Report of the commissioners appointed to enquire into famine in Bengal and Orissa (1866), Vol.I, p. 8.
18. R. C. Dutta, Economic history of India, Vols. II (Delhi, 1963) p.128.
19. W. W. Hunter, A Statistical account of Bengal, Cuttack and Balasore, Vol.XVIII, 1877, pp. 173-174.
20. Maddox Report (1986-1900 A.D.) Vol. I, p.7.
21. Maddox Report, op.cit., p.8.
22. Utkal Dipika, 11 January, 1873.
23. Ibid, 8 March, 1873.
24. Annual administration report of the Bengal presidency for the year 1879-80.
25. Report on the land revenue settlement of Sambalpur district in central province, 1855-89, Calcutta, 1890, p.11.
26. L.S.S.O.' Malley, Sambalpur District Gazetteers, Calcutta 1909, pp. 160-162.
27. N. N. Benerjee, Report on the agriculture of the district of Cuttack, 1898, p. 143.
28. J. F. W. James, Final report on the revision settlement of Orissa, 1906-12, pp.7-8.
29. Utkal Dipika, 20 January, 1928.
30. Utkal Dipika., 23 August, 1873.
31. Utkal Dipika., 29 May, 1876.
32. Utkal Dipika, 29 April, 1874.
33. Maddox Report (1890-1900), Vol. I, pp.29-30.
34. Annual administration report of the Orissa division (1888-89), pp.37-38.
35. Annual administration report of Orissa division, (1885-88), pp.47-48.
36. General administration report of Orissa division, (1885-88), pp.47-48.
37. Ibid. (1888-89) pp. 37-38.
38. Ibid. pp. 37-38.
39. General administration report of Orissa division,

(1888-89), p.42.
40. Ibid. p.42.
41. Maddox Report (1890-1900), Vol. I, p.29.
42. GAROD (1894-95) From Mr. H. G. Cooke, Commissioner of Orissa division No. 1059, Cuttack, 5 July 1895.
43. AGAR of Orissa division 1894-95 from Mr. H. G. Cooke, C.S.I., Commissioner, Orissa division No. 1059 dated 05.07.1895, p. 49.
44. General administration report of Orissa division, (1898-99), p. 41.
45. P. N. Chopra, B. N. Puri, M. N. Das. A Social Cultural and Economic history of India, The Macmillan Company of India Ltd. (1974) pp. 196-197.
46. Dharmkumar, T. Raichaudhury, The Cambridge Economic history of India, Vol.II (1757-1970) Cambridge University Press, (1982). p. 737.
47. Utkal Dipika, Part-XIII, 23 March, 1878, No. 21.
48. Utkal Dipika, 28 February, 1880, No.9.
49. T. E. Ravenshaw to Secretary, Government of Bengal, No. 271, 23 July, 1873, Para-118, General administration report of the Orissa division for 1872-73.
50. Utkal Dipika, 2 January, 1875.
51. Utkal Dipika, 23 March, 1878.
52. Administration report of the Orissa division, 1879-80, p.89.
53. C. E. Buckland, Bengal under the Lt. Governor, Vol.II, p.700-701.
54. Report of estimate and correspondence of Benaras, Cuttack, Puri, Railway, 1883-84, pp. 64-70.
55. Peter Hannethy, Crop Trend in central province in India, 1861-1921, Vol.II, Part-3, p.351.
56. S. L. Maddox, Report on the settlement of the province of Orissa, 1890-1900, Part-I, Calcutta,

1900, p. 9.
57. Bengal revenue proceeding (separate revenue), Excise Deptt., Commissioner of Excise, Bengal presidency to the Board of Revenue lower province, 11 Nov., 1897.
58. Indian Industrial Commission (minute of evidences) 1916-17, Bengal and Central province, Vol.II, Calcutta, 1918, pp. 770-773.
59. Quinquennial administration report of the Orissa division, 1900-1901 to 1904-05, p.36.
60. Basic Railway Statistics of India, 1948, No. STS-16(3) 48, New Delhi, 1949, p.137.
61. G. V. Joshi, Writings and speaches (Poona, 1912), p. 699.
62. G. S. Lyre, Quoted by Statesman, 31 May, 1905.
63. W. W. Hunter, Statistical account of Bengal, Vol.XIX, London. 1877, p.263.
64. Ibid, p. 263.
65. Report on the administration of Bengal, 1883-84, Calcutta, 1884, p.14.
66. K.S. Behera, "Maritime Trade in Ancient Orissa" in sidelights on History and Culture of Orissa, Cuttack 1977, pp. 113-115.
67. Report of the Orissa Famine Commission (1866), Vol.I, Part-II, Para-30.
68. Annual administration report of Bengal presidency for the year 1878-79, Calcutta, 1879, p. 109.
69. C. E. Buckland, Bengal under Lt. Governors, Vol.I, Calcutta, 1902, p. 394.
70. Ibid, p. 394.
71. Report on the administration of Customs, Deptt. of Bengal presidency, 1874-75, Secy. V, Para-97, Bengal Revenue Proceedings, Nov. 1875.
72. Utkal Dipika, 20 January 1872.
73. J. Beams, Memories of Bengal Civilian (New Delhi, 1979), p.231.
74. T. J. Maltby, The Ganjam district manual,

Madras, 1918, p. 33.

75. Ibid. p. 31.
76. Thomas Motte, Early European Travellers in Nagpur territories, p. 16.
77. W. W. Hunter, History of Orissa, Vol. II, London, 1878, p. 65.
78. J. H. Hurd, Railways and Expansion of Markets in India, 1861-1921, EEH, Dec. 1975.

Chapter - 3

INLAND TRADE

Production and distribution of economic goods are based on the co-existence and at times, inter-penetration of a subsistence. The bulk of the population in Orissa lived in the villages and the bulk of their needs for goods was satisfied through production for use and reciprocal exchanges. The exchange of goods was found at virtually every level & spehere of economic life. The dominance of subsistence oriented production was modified by surpluses and deficits necessiating multitiered and multi-faceted commerical activity[1] Inland trade might be purely intra-local, confined to one particular producing unit, village or town or inter-local, between different villages and towns. Generally speaking, the trend of the movement of goods was from the village or group of villages to towns. But the village was not actualy self-sufficient in all its needs which were partly supplied through the rural markets.[2] So inland trade formed one of the keys for the business activity of the state.

The inland trade of Orissa was quite unsatisfactory for a long time. The reasons behind this miserable condition of inland trade in Orissa were many. Firstly, Orissa was very backward in matters of roads and other means of communications.[3] Secondly, very small number of local people participated in trade. A major portion of it was controlled by the outsiders such as Bengali, Marwari, Telugu and merchants of Bombay.[4] Thirdly, almost all the trade and business were conducted by the barter system for a long time.[5] Fourthly, salt which was an important article of trade in Orissa was monopolised by the British government.[6] Fifthly, due to dreadful climate and the inaccessible forests and hilly regions of the state, trade was confined only to the dry seasons.[7] Sixthly, monopoly in trade was in vogue in most of the zamindari and Garhjat states of Orissa. According to this practice, in lieu of an annual tax to the kings treasury a trader was appointed to deal with a particular commodity or commodities which must be sold to him by the producers under compulsion. Under this system, the producer must receive the price that the commissioned tradesmen thought right to offer and none was allowed to enter the market except the monopolist.[8] Added to this, the Rajas and Maharajas of these states of Orissa collected custom duties known as 'sayar' for every article of commerce. This was collected at choukey or custom stations situated at strategic places of the states. This discouraged the traders of Orissa to a considerable extent.[9] Seventhly, the people of Orissa have little fascination for trade and commerce. The tribals who formed a sizeable portion of the population of Orissa detested trade and considered it as a degrading occupation.[10] Moreover, most of the people were extremely poor and they had not enough money to invest in trade. But with the opening of railways in 1890 trade of Orissa was revolutionised and business was intensified.

Road-Borne Trade

Inland trade was carried on by means of pack-bullocks, carts, for a long time. But from the 90's of the last century trains were utilised for the purpose of trade. The inland trade was carried on with central provinces, Bengal, Orissa Garhjat states and the Madras districts.[11] Bullock carts drawn by bullocks and buffaloes were extensively used for the purpose of trade and commerce. These carts generally carried 10 maunds of Cuttack weight.[12] For the purpose of inland transport elephants, buffaloes and asses were also used. But packhorses were used extensively for covering long distance and for carrying merchandise.

The inland trade of Orissa was carried on mainly by outside (Bengali, Marwari, Telugu and Bombay) traders and partly by a class of local men. The outside traders from Raipur, Bombay, Calcutta, Andhra and other parts of India travelled from village to village and even penetrated into the innermost recesses of the bills and bartered their goods for the produce of the soil.[13] They used to come from January to April forming themselves into caravans for better security of their property.[14] There were some foreign traders who purchased grains and forest products when the prices were low and exported to their godowns at Cuttack either by carts or by boats through the river Mahanadi. They generally made advances of money to the Paikars of middle man for purchasing agricultural and forest products. They also imported many useful foreign goods and carried them in the carts or pack-bullocks to the different markets where they found a ready sale.[15]

The growth of communications and transport and the establishment of markets in central places provided stimulus to internal and external trade. There was no long roads deserving the name till 1880 except the Cuttack trunk road (Calcutta to Madras boarder at Barkul) and Jagannath road (from Raipur to Puri via Sohela, Barpali, Binka, Sonepur, Barmula, Banki and Cuttack) and some local roads. But with the establishment of local bodies like district boards, local boards after 1882, the development of road system was given great impetus. One of the main functions of these local bodies was the management and construction of the roads. The roads could be divided under three categories, namely metal roads, unmetalled roads and village roads.

Some roads of importance which might be regarded as provincial roads were grand trunk road, cuttack - sonepur road and cuttack - sambalpur road. The grand trunk road which was the highway from Midnapur in Bengal to Ganjam in Madras presidency was metalled and crossed the river Baitarani, Kharsuan, Brahmani, Mahanadi and Rusikulya by ferries. The other two provincial roads which ran through the valley of Mahanadi and princely states were neither metalled nor bridged.[16] The most important trade routes were cuttack-khurda road, pipli - khurda road, bhadrak - chandabali road, sambalpur - raipur road and sambalpur-jharsuguda road. The surplus produce of rice of the four districts (Cuttack, Puri, Balasore and Sambalpur) was sent for export through these roads.[17] Though these roads were unmetalled and not properly bridged, still then the traffic on these roads was very heavy in winter. These roads were commercial and pilgrim roads used by the pilgrims from central provinces to Puri and the traders from Raipur and Nagpur to Orissa.

Though transport system was not developed in Orissa but partly it stimulated internal and external trade improved the organisation of industry, low rate the cost of production and expanded the market economy after the famine of 1866. The gap between industrial and agricultural sector was bridged through communication. There was no means of ascertaining the total quantity of merchandise - imported and exported by road, but there was little doubt that this was much larger than the rail borne imports and exports.

Water-Borne Trade

Rivers formed the great highways of Orissa especially during the rainy season. When the roads of Orissa were impossible for wheel traffic, being muddy and unbridged, the great rivers namely Mahanadi, Brahmani, Salandi, Dhamra, Kushabhadra, Bhargavi, Daya, Kathjori, Suvarnarekha, Baitarani, Rushikulya, Bahuda and Goberi supplied an easy means of communication for import and export of commodities.

River Mahanadi was the chief water route between Cuttack and Sambalpur and the princely states of Orissa like Athgarh, Athmallik, Banki, Baramba, Boud, Daspalla, Khandapara and Narasinghpur. River Mahanadi was the main outlet for the trade of Orissa till the opening of railways, boats could ascend the Mahanadi as far as Arang of Madhya Pradesh. During floods boats took five days to reach Cuttack from Sambalpur, while the journey to Sonepur lasted for one day and to Binka only six hours. But the duration of the return journey was much longer. In July it took twentyfive days for loaded boats to reach Sambalpur from Cuttack.[18]

River Brahmani was the broad waterway for the people of Deograh sub-division of Sambalpur and the Talcher and Dhenkanal state for nearly 8 months in a year.[19] River Baitarani was an important artery of communication for the people of Jajpur sub-division and Keonjhar state. In dry seasons also it was navigable by small boats as far as Anandpur. A considerable trade was carried on at this place.[20] River Rusikulya was the main outlet of trade of Ganjam district. During the rains timber and bamboo trade was carried on through the river Rushikulya. The timbers from the Sorada forest were transported by this river as far as Ganjam town. Bamboos were also transported on the river Bahuda extensively during the rains. The only water-borne trade of Koraput district was the transport of the bamboo of Malkangiri by the Sileru and Rajmuhendry.[21]

The three great rivers of the Puri district, the Kushbhadra, Bhargavi and Daya were navigable for several months of the year. Even in the hot weather country boats could be seen along their banks for atleast ten miles above the point where these rivers enter the Chilka. The boats belonged chiefly to Ganjam traders, who brought loads of bamboo and other goods and in return carried the surplus rice of the southern part of the district. They used to come via the Ganjam canal and the Chilka lake, which was available for boat traffic round the year.[22]

For the purpose of export and import to the hinter land of Orissa, some canals were constructed. The canals were very useful in carrying export trade. Prominent among those canal, Taladanda canal, Machagaon canal, High level canal, Jajpur canal, Gobri canal, Dudhei canal and Coast canal.[23]

Navigation through these rivers was conducted by country boats and rafts. Regarding the boats Thomas Motte writes, "These boats were light, the plank being only an inch thick and timbers small in proportion could carry from 600 to 700 maunds." The largest boat was 40 feet long and 4 feet wide."[24] But, Hunter has described these boats as flat-bottomed and were able to carry about 25 tons of burden.[25] The boats used in the Chilka lake were quite peculiar. They were made of planks without ribs or keels and were perfectly flat-bottomed with perpendicular sides. This form was necessary in the unimproved state of the landing places as the lake was very shallow at the edges, except where as rock knoll formed the bank and in such position goods could not be landed with safety from the breaking of the waves. Produces were brought through the Chilka lake at Rambha, Parikuda and Malud.[26]

Transportation through these water routes especially during the rains was extensive because it was less expensive and there was no fear of way-side robberers and wild animals as in land routes. But since the opening of railways, the construction of bridges over the rivers and metalled roads, the river-borne trade had greatly diminished.

Rail-Borne Trade

Railways played an important role in the inland trade of Orissa. After the opening of railways in 1890, the trade of Orissa was really revolutionised. The opening of railways resulted in a large influx of traders who penetrated into the interiors of Orissa to trade in agriculture and forest products.

The main line of the south-eastern railway which traverses the Bamra and Sambalpur subdivisions was opened in 1890-91. The branch line from Jharsuguda to Sambalpur which extended upto Titlagarh and joined the Raipur-Vijayanagaram was opened in 1893.[27] In 1895 the railway line from Rambha to Berhampur was opened. The line from Khurda to Rambha was opened on March 1896. A branch line from khurda road station to Puri was opened in traffic in 1901. The Nuapada-Gunupur narrow gauge (a branch of S.E. railways) was completed in 1900. The Paralakhemundi light railway which was constructed by the Maharaja Krushna Chandra Gajapati of Paralakhemundi (from Paralakhemundi to Gunupur) was opened for traffic on 1st April, 1900.[28]

The rail head towns served as the main outlet for the export and import of goods. Jatni (Khurda road station) was the famous rail head which served as the main outlet for the agricultural and allied produce drawn from Nayagarh, Khandapara, Ranpur, Daspalla, Pipli, Nimapara, Gop, Khurda, Delanga and Begunia areas. Coconut which was one of the important cash crops of Puri district accounted for more than 50% of the states coconut production Sakhigopal, Delang, Pipli, Kanas, Brahmagiri, Krushna Prasad, Balianta, Ballipatna, Nimapara, Gop, Kakatpur and Astaranga had big coconut orchards. Coconut was exported in large quantities to West Bengal, Bihar, Madhya Pradesh and Andhra Pradesh. Sakhigopal and Delang railway stations were the chief stations of exporting coconuts.[29] Betel-nut and betel-leaf which were grown abundantly in and around the Puri town, were exported in large quantities through these railway stations. Besides, Puri district had the biggest lake in the country viz. the Chilka on the east coast. More than 150 varieties of sea-fish were found in the lake, Prawn, Crabs and Mullets which constituted on an average 45 to 50 percent of the catch were regularly exported to Calcutta[30] by train from Balugaon and Chilka stations.

The english traveller T. Motte mentions that Sambalpur was famous for its cottage industries and was the centre of trade and commerce.[31] The rail head towns of Sambalpur district viz. Sambalpur, Jharsuguda, Ibid, Baragarh, Brajarajnagar, Belpahar, Titlagarh, Bagdihi, Dhutra were the main centres of import and export of commodities.[32]

The railway stations of Ganjam district like Khalikote, Rambha, Huma, Ganjam, Chhatrapur, Jagannathpur, Surala and Nuapada served as the main outlet for the export of salt, fish (both fresh and dired), agricultural and jungle products.[33]

The saal timber which was in great demand for the construction of gun carriage and railways was another important item of export to Calcutta and Madras. Mr. Hurton has been employed by the British government as the agent in Orissa to supply saal timber to Madras since 1842.[34] From the Nowrangpur taluk saal sleepers were exported by cart to Kantabanji railway stations and then to Madras. The saal sleepers were exported by cart to the rail head towns of Orissa and then to Calcutta and Madras by trains. The above account reveals that, the imports by rail were few but export were larger in quantity and were varied in kind.

ARTICLES OF EXPORT AND IMPORT

Articles of Export

The development of roads, railways, navigable canals and ports facilitated export and import trade by providing mobility of people to move to different places. The articles of export and import varied from district to district and place to place. Rice was the staple export all over the districts of Orissa.

The chief exports from the district of Cuttack were rice, oil seeds, hides, jute, timber, horns, feathers, silvers, filigree works, etc. Agricultural products of permanently settled estates like Kanika, Kujang, Darpan, Aul, etc. were brought to cuttack for sale to the merchants coming from Madras, Bombay, Ceylon, Laccadive, Maldive islands and other european countries.[35] Cuttack town earned a world wide reputation in filigree works. Specimen of this filigree works were displayed in the european exhibition mainly exported from cuttack market.[36] Forest products such as murobalam, lac, wax, vomica and resin collected from different parts were exported to Calcutta and Madras.[37]

Articles of export from Balasore district were rice, cotton, oil seeds, hides, jute, horns, feathers, tobacco, garlic, brass-metal, salt, fish and dired fish, etc. Brass-metal was produced at Remuna.[38] Salt was also exported to different places from the aurangs of Balasore districts.

The exports of the Puri district were quite different. It exported the largest varieties of fish and dried fish, coconut, betel-nut and betel-leaf and tussar cloth to different parts of Orissa and outside Orissa. Brass and bell-metal utensils, degchis and ornaments were made in considerable quantities at Balakati and Kantillo which were exported to different parts of Orissa, West Bengal, Bihar, Assam and Madhya Pradesh.[39] The other principal exports were gram, pulses and unrefined sugar. Nearly the whole of the export and import trade of this district was done by the railway after 1890's.

Thus, the chief articles of export from different districts of Orissa were paddy, rice, hide, ghee, bidi leaves, oil seeds, fish, dried fish, coconut, betel-leaves and other forest products.

Articles of Import

Imports were much less than the exports of goods in all the districts of Orissa. This was because the wants of the people during this period under review were limited and they were usually contented with whatever little they produced or procure easily. Import trade of the Cuttack and Balasore district were same during the period under review. The principal articles of import from Calcutta were fancy goods, kerosene oil, crockery, glass-ware, potatoes, lead, copper, zinc, gold, silver and cotton yarn.[40] The articles of import from other places were salt, turmeric, chilli, sugar and tobacco leaves from Ganjam, coconuts and coconut oil and salted fish from

Puri and wheat, pulses, oil-seeds, cotton and molasses from the central provinces.[41] Similarly, the articles of import from Puri district were kerosene oil, spices, cotton goods, salt and several jungle products.

Thus, coal, hardware, vegetables, kerosene oil, petrol, cotton goods, betel nuts, spices, mustard oil, coconut oil, gunny bags, salt, sugar, matches and tobacco were the chief imported articles where as rice, paddy, dried fish, bidi leaves, ghee and jungle products were the chief articles of export from Orissa during the period under review.

Trade centres and Markets

Trade centres and markets played a very important role in the trade of Orissa. There existed no regular markets in Orissa at the time of British conquest. Every village was a self-sufficient unit. Whatever a particular village community could not produce according to their need they usually depended on the neighbouring villages for that. Gradually, numerous trade centres, weekly and bi-weekly markets were established throughout Orissa. There were some trade centres and weekly markets which had inter-state transactions. Thousands of people from different places congregated in these markets for the sale and purchase of their goods and cattles.

For a detailed study of marts and markets, the following heads may be adopted.

1. Trade centres
2. Cattle markets

3. Weekly markets or hats

4. Bi-weekly markets or village hats

5. Annual fair markets or melas

Trade centres

Goods imported from outside alongwith those produced in the locality were distributed through various trade centres of Orissa. In the district of Cuttack, Robert Ker, Magistrate, Cuttack, suggested to the Bengal government for opening of regular markets as a basic support of the commercial prosperity of this country. On getting recommendations, government granted lease of lands to intending merchants of Cuttack town to open shops in the town and Cuttack sprang up as an important regular commercial centre during 19th century.[42] Agricultural products, hides, and filigree works had the reputation. Besides Cuttack, there were a number of trade centres. Jajpur, Jagatsinghpur, Kendrapara, Banki, Chatia, Pattamundai, Chandikhole, Jajpur road, Dharmasala, Hajipur and Tirtol were other centres of trade and commerce[43] with the opening of Coast canal, Taladanda canal, Kendrapara canal, development of false-point, Chandabali port and the opening of railways facilitated commercial activities of Cuttack district.

Trade centres of Balasore district were Balasore, Bhadrak, Jaleswar, Chandabali, Bhograi, Remuna, Basta and Baliapal. Development of ports communications accelerated the commercial activities of the district to the hinter lands.

Marketing system was not modern in Puri during the time of British conquest. Puri town could only give commercial facility because the pilgrims visited Puri. Towards the close of the 19th century ports of Puri were abandoned and salt manufacture was stopped, for which government did not pay much attention for the development of markets. The principal centres of business both wholesale and retail transactions of Puri district were Puri, Jatni, Khurda, Balugaon, Banpur, Pipli, Gop, Itamati and Astarang. Khurda remained as an important business centre till the opening of the East Coast railway line when the centre was shifted to the railway station at Jatni.[44] Merchants of tributary mahals used to visit, Balakati regularly to collect brass utensils.[45]

Cattle Markets

There were some markets or hats in Orissa which were exclusively meant for the sale and purchase of animals and birds. These markets usually sat once in a week and established in different places of Orissa. Professional cattle dealers used to go to different markets to bring herds of cattle, mostly bullocks and cows for sale. At Pattamundai, Indupur and Chhatia of Cuttack district large cattle markets sat once in every week. Weekly cattle markets were held at Bhadrak, Balasore, Chandabali, Basudevpur, Jaleswar and Bhograi of Balasore district. Delanga, Brahmagiri, Balugaon, Nirakarpur and Begunia of Puri district were the venues of cattle markets.[46]

Weekly Markets or Hats

In rural areas a greater part of the local trade was carried on at weekly markets or hats scattered throughout Orissa. These hats sat between sunrise to sunset. These markets, though generally not of any great size were conveniently situated for the supply of local needs. They also acted as centres where grain was collected for export. At these villages weekly markets the villagers disposed of their surplus stocks of rice, pulses and local produce and purchased cotton or piece goods, utensils, kerosene, salt, fancy-articles, etc. The weekly markets were the most important channels of agricultural marketing in Orissa. The village weekly markets were of great importance to tribals since they sold their produce in exchange of their daily necessities and luxuries. Merchants from town areas of Orissa and outside visited these markets for purchasing goods at cheaper rate.

Bi-weekly markets or village hats

There were also many bi-weekly markets in Orissa. These markets or village hats sat twice in a week. These markets were very useful to the rural folk because the articles of daily necessities and luxuries were not available in every village. These markets were of great importance to the scheduled castes and scheduled tribes because they exchanged their produce for the articles of daily consumption. These markets sat at a distance of 10 to 15 km. Thus the average distance covered by the people to reach the nearest market centre was approximately 10 to 15 kms.

Annual Fair or Mela markets

Thousands of people used to assemble at the different fairs or melas to enjoy the celebrations, pay their devotion and offerings to the deities. Therefore, a sort of hats or markets sat in these religious places. A certain amount of trade in grain, utensils, clothes and other household articles were transacted at these annual fairs or melas. These type of markets were held at Narsinghnath and Humma in Sambalpur, Remuna and Ardi in Balasore, Dhabaleswar, Cuttack, Chandikhole, Jajpur and Olasuni in Cuttack, Puri badanda and old Bhubaneswar in Puri district. A great deal of local trade was carried on at these religious gatherings and festivals.

Thus, trade and commerce of Orissa were carried out by internal markets. T.E. Ravenshaw noticed it as "a market feature in this part of India". The number of weekly markets in different districts was as follows : Cuttack - 279, Puri - 55 and Balasore - 165.[47] There were few capitalists in the province. The internal trade was chiefly conducted by Marwaris, while outside trade was almost entirely in the hands of some enterprising muslims from Kutch and Bombay.[48]

Currency and Coinage

Trade was directly connected with the currency problems. During the Maratha government and in earlier times also, Kauries - the little white glossy shells (cypraea moneta) were the chief medium of exchange in Orissa.[49] They were mainly imported from the Maldive islands.[50] Kauries were used in monetary transactions from an early time in Orissa. On one occasion Narasingh Dev, the Raja of Orissa (1622-1646) granted 91,538 kahanas of Kauries for white washing the temple of Jagannath.[51] From the diaries of Streynsham master it appears that merchants used Kauries for their business.[52]

But it is not known yet definitely when and how the cowry shells came to serve as a medium of exchange in India and Orissa. The brave sailors of Kalinga (modern Orissa) known as Sadhava carried on maritime trade with the far off islands like Burma, Ceylon, Java, Sumatra, etc. Thomas Bowery in the 17th century A.D. found cowry shells as the only coin known to the villagers of Orissa. Andrew Hamilton in the 18th century A.D. records that cowry was being exchanged with cloth, rice and butter. Thus, there were evidences of the prevalence of cowry currency in Orissa from the 8th century A.D. to the beginning of the 19th century.[53]

The cowry currency maintained the government rate of exchange of four kahanas and two pans to the rupee in the market till 1808 and then fell as low as seven kahanas per rupee in the Cuttack district in 1812.[54] During the first phase of the British rule the scarcity of kauris was felt as the army people were paid heavy through Kauris. At this critical movement, the pilgrims visiting Lord Jagannath were pressing hard for Kauri currency.[55] This was also evident from the letter to Harcourt to Mr. Shaw, private secretary to the Governor General "we are very much distressed for want of small coins or Kauris."[56]

British government introduced their own coins known as sicca rupee or silver rupee in 1808. Such sicca rupee or silver rupee was divided into 16 annas and each anna was further divided into 6 paises. Paises were also subdivided into pice. Eight anna, four anna, one anna and half anna and one paise coins were introduced by the British government under this system. These British coins were also known as Murshidabad sicca coins. Thus the British government introduced a uniform coinage system throughout India. Coins of East India company as well as coins bearing the portraits of British monarch were in circulation during the period under review. Revenue was collected entirely in silver coins soon after its introduction in 1808. The collection of silver at the Jagannath in 1807 was of Rs. 1,17,000 while it had always varied between Rs. 38,400 and Rs. 70,410 in previous years.[57]

The hasty step to stop the cowry currency which constituted the main medium of exchange among the vast majority of the people for centuries resulted in an abnormal fall in the price of cowry upsetting the whole monetary system. It caused a great misery and hardship to the people at large, prices of things rose high in Kauries. The government rate of exchange was four kahanas and two pans to the rupee. But the market rate of exchange was about seven kahanas to the rupee. Thus, this state of affairs brought hardships to ryots. Probably this discontent was one of the reasons why the people joined in the rebellion of 1817.[58]

The question of currency became difficult because at the beginning it did not receive proper attention from the British government. In the words of Ewer, "the question of the cowry currency escaped altogether the notice of the commissioners, Messers Buller and Richardson, was not thought by those gentleman worthy of any considerations.[59] The result was that the rice trade suffered and the total export fell from 5,45,000 mounds to 2,85,000 between 1808 to 1815.[60] The decline in trade had serious consequences over the general economic life of the province.

The prosperity of industry and the growth of trade and commerce was directly connected with the currency system. Whatever may be the consequences of British coinage system in Orissa, they were responsible for the promulgation of a uniform system of currency in Orissa.

Weights and Measures

Prior to the enforcement of the metric system of weights and measures trade was transacted only through the indigenous weights and measures. But the weights and measures that were in practice in Orissa during the British period varied from place to place.[61] The seer was the most common system of weight. But was also varied so much that, it was scarcely found to be the same at any two districts of Orissa. In rural areas people used dry measures like Mana, Tambi and Nauti in all transactions of rice, paddy and other foodgrains. All these measures varied not only in nomenclature but also in capacities from area to area. Materials from which these measures were constructed also varied from place to place. In some parts brass measures were in use and in other measures were prepared from earth. As a result of such differences in the use of dry measures there was ample scope for the trader to cheat the producers. With regard to seer weights also, difficulties were experienced by the traders in inter-state transactions as these weights varied from state to state and from district to district.[62] Adda (64 tolas of fine rice) and sera (105 tolas in Cuttack and 80 tolls in Puri and other areas) were commonly accepted for measuring dry grains. Following weights were in practice in Ganjam district.

15 tolas made 1 sola

4 solas made 1 adda

4 addas made 1 gouni of tum

4 tum made 1 nauti or 12 seers or 80 tolas

For measuring length, rod or nala was in use. One nala was equal to 13 feet. The local land measurement was 5 bharanas equal to one acre and 20 nauties consituted one bharana. Thus, bharana was both a unit of area and volume.[63]

In the gradation of counting, 4 units made one ganda, 20 ganda made one pana and 16 panas made a kahan. There were also separate volume measures for liquids. Liquids were weighed according to the standard seer. Adda, Boda, Sola and Adha were also in use in some areas. Bhari, Tola, Rati and Masa were the weights for gold and silver. The measure of length of mill-made cloths was the standard yard gaj or 36 inches divided into 16 giras. But for measuring country-made cloth, the unit of length was hata or cubit of 18 inches, and chakhanda or half cubit.[64] For weighing vegetables, turmeric, fish and brass utensils, the unit was the bisa, which was equivalent to 27 palas (it varied from 20 to 27 palas in different parts of Orissa) one pala was equal to 6 tolas.

The following table shows the old weights and measures and their equivalent in metric units.

Old units	***Metric equivalent***
1 tola	11.664 grams
1 seer (of 89 tolas)	9.993 kg.
1 maund	0.37 quintal
Tumba (240 tolas)	2.800 grams

Bisa (30 palas)	2.100 grams
Adda (60 tolas)	0.700 grams
Boda (30 tolas)	0.350 grams
Mana (120 tolas)	1.400 grams

In addition the following weights and measures were commonly used in Orissa :

Mass	8 ratis
Tola or Bhari	12 masas
Chhatak	5 tolas
Seer	80 tolas
Maund	40 seers[65]
Length hata	Length of a cubit roughly 1/2 feet
Chakhanda	1/2 of hat or 9 inches
Gira	1/16 yard
Kos	2 miles
Mile	1/2 kms. roughly[66]

Modern and matric system of weights and measures were not introduced in Orissa during the period under review. There was no system to verify and check these weights and measures. So these measures varied not only in nomenclature but also in capacities from area to area and the buyers, were generally cheated. Besides, the traders were in difficulties while transactions were made between two districts or two states. As a result, there was ample scope for the traders to cheat the people. It also led to several problems in inter-state transactions.

PRICE OF COMMODITIES

The rise and fall of prices of commodities were inter-linked and inter-related with its availability and scarcity. It very much depended on the rainfall and weather. When the rainfall was even and copious and there was no other natural calamities and impesticides, the prices of difference commodities remained reasonable but when the reverse was the case the prices of goods increased. Besides that, when the goods were imported in large quantities from Orissa, the prices were increased in that year. Because of all these factors the prices of commodities varied from place to place and year to year.

When Orissa was visited by a terrible famine of most desolating character in 1866 there was scarcity of rice. So the price of rice soared high. In August 1866 one could purchase $4\frac{1}{2}$ seer of rice tax one rupee in Cuttack.[67]

Since rice cultivation was the easiest means of cultivation it covered most of the cropped area. The winter rice alone covered 70%, 77% and 75% of the total cropped area of Cuttack, Puri and Balasore districts, respectively.[68] This is one of the principal cause of the growth of market for rice both inside and outside the province. The cheap rate of rice stimulated rice trade between Orissa and Calcutta in the first half of the 19th century and between Orissa and Madras in the second half of 19th century.[69]

The following table shows the price of rice between 1836 - 1898 in Cuttack.

Year	***Rice in seers***
1836	43

1840	21
1844	54
1848	59
1852	54
1856	44
1860	23
1864	33
1866	13
1868	31
1872	26
1876	20
1880	19
1884	19
1888	20
1892	13
1896	18
1898	14[70]

(Source : Annual Report on the survey and settlement of the province of Orissa. Vol. I, Calcutta, 1900, p. 199)

In 1880, 44 seers of rice per rupee was available in Sambalpur whereas only 19 seers of rice was available in Cuttack in the same year for the same amount. This proves that, the prices of foodgrains differed from place to place.[71]

The next table shows the price of essential articles between 1836-1898.

AVERAGE OF 1811 - 1817

Name of articles	*Price per maund Rs. As. Ps.*	*In 1899 Rs. As. Ps.*
Biri	0-15-6	2-4-6
Arhar	1-14-6	2-12-0
Ghee	15-0-0	22-0-0
Cotton yard	43-0-0 to 85-0-0	16-0-0 to 40-0-0
Sugar	8-8-0	4-12-0 to 8-8-0
Tobacco	5-0-0	15-0-0
Betelnut	7-0-0	7-0-0
Kerosene	9-10-0	5-0-0
Coconut oil	21-8-0	15-8-0
Salt	3-4-0	3-10-0[72]

The price rise of essential food stuffs proved fatal to the interest of marginal farmers without stock of grain for scarcity season. Increased quantum of import of consumer goods increased the wants of marginal farmers while heavy export of rice raised the prices of essential food stuffs making indebtedness and indispensable feature of their life.

Mercantile Classes

Mercantile classes who were engaged in the trade of Orissa were mostly outsiders. Very small number of local people participated in trade. But these mercantile classes were different from district to district and areas to areas. All the business of import and export to and from Cuttack.

Balasore districts were managed by Bengali,

Marwari, Telegu and merchants of Bombay and Mahammadan. The business of Sambalpur district was controlled by Marwari, Nagpur and Raipur merchants. Almost all the business of import and export to and from the districts of Ganjam, Puri and Koraput districts were managed by the Kumutis and Bengalis. The telugu kumutis who were living in the southern part of the Ganjam district and the plains of Vizagpatam district made periodic trips or sent their agents to different areas for the purchase of goods. They also penetrated into the hills to purchase the jungle products and see the loading and despatching of the carts and lorries which had come up from the lower country to take down the goods.[73] They also organised the operations of the gang of brinjaris who drove pack bullocks between Ganjam and central provinces furnishing them with loads of salt to take to the hinterland and giving them commissions for purchases of grain to be made in return.

The Mahammadan community also played a part in the trade of Ganjam and Koraput district, especially in the hide trade. The Bombay firm of Haji Jamal Nur Mahammad, which had a branch at Jaypore, probably handled more merchandise on hide trade than any other places of south Orissa.[74]

The outside traders from Nagpur, Raipur, Calcutta, Bombay and other parts of India travelled from village to village even penetrated into the innermost recesses of the hills and bartered their goods for the produce of the soil. They brought umbrella, lantern, torch-light, knife, readymade dresses to Orissa. They used to come from the month of January to April forming themselves into caravans for better security of their property and bringing their goods on bullocks or horses.[75]

There were some outside traders who purchased grains and forest produce when the prices were low and exported to Cuttack either by carts or boats and then to their destinations. They generally made advance of money to the paikars or middle man for purchase of agricultural and forest products. They also imported many useful foreign goods, carried them in the carts or pack-bullocks to the different markets and hats (weekly markets) where they found ready sale.[76]

Money lending was also a lucrative profession of some trading classes. The oriya sundis and the telugu kumutis were its chief practitioners. They visited the different districts of Orissa during the dry seasons peddled petty goods, let out small amounts and recovered their debts with interest in the following year.[77]

Thus, trade was carried on principally by outside traders and partly by a class of local men. The Banjaras, Marwaris, Bengalis, Telugu kumutis, Bombay and Nagpur merchants were the outside traders. The Oriya sundis, oriya kumutis, marwaris of Cuttack and Sambalpur district, the banias of Cuttack and the muslims of Orissa formed the class of local traders. From the above analysis it is clear that, a major portion of the trade was controlled by the outsiders and very small number of the local people participated in it.

IMPACT OF INLAND TRADE ON THE ECONOMY OF ORISSA

When Orissa was conquered by East India company in 1803, it had no basic infrastructure or facilities for trade. Orissa was said to be roadless at the time of British conquest. The East India company did not pay any heed to the construction of highways and roads in Orissa. The great famine of 1866 showed how isolated was Orissa from the outside world especially during the monsoons.

Added to this, - the East India company introduced salt monopoly in Orissa. The monopoly of salt trade seriously affected the poor people. The price of salt was arbitrarily fixed in the days of the company and was so high at all times that, it was a source of vexation to the poor. The crown's government abandoned salt monopoly in 1836 and introduced excise on licence system. At the same time, salt was supplied at a lower price because of the importation of Liverpool salt. The local salt, manufactured under excise or licence system could not be sold at a cheaper rate than the imported salt of a superior type. As a result, the local manufacture had declined. Thus, the salt industry which supplied livelihood to 20,000 families in Orissa was ruined.

Orissa was famous for weaving industry. Tassar and cotton cloths were made by handloom in many places, some of which were prized for their fine texture and durability. But this cottage industry did not thrive in the face of competition with cheaper imported fabrics from Manchester. Thus, died an industry which supported a large number of people. The concentration of people on the land was aggravated because of the decay of these two industries.

While the destruction of local industries forced the masses to take up agriculture as the only means of support, the iniquitious land revenue policy and the vagaries of nature filled the cup of their misery. The enhancement of the rent, imposition of illegal cases and absentee landlordism proved harmful to the tenants.

The frequent crop failures on account of flood or drought plunged the ryots in debt to mahajan or zamindaras. They seldom managed to recover from that. Orissa was the only province of Bengal which lacked government's incentive for promoting trade and commercialisation of agriculture. Even the zamindars for fear of increased revenue discovered cash crop cultivation. Under these circumstances, Orissa remained mainly a rice producing tract. This proneness to monoculture in place of diversified profession broke down the self-sustained village economy and caused massive pressure of population on land. The declining weaving industry and salt manufacture for its lack of profitability after 1833 Charter Act led to import of machine made commodities. As a result rice remained the only major exportable commodity. But the total cost of export of rice was unequal to that of importation of consumer goods. Besides this imbalance between export and import, massive export of rice made the economy vulnerable to any strain caused by famine and scarcity when price of rice went beyond the purchasing power of the ordinary producers. Even in normal years of harvest famine conditions prevailed due to shortage of foodgrains and high price of rice and other food item.

Rise in prices affected the fate of the overwhelming number of the population who sunk below the subsistence level. Moreover, frequent variations in rainfall causing natural calamities broke down the saving capacity of the people and made money lending an integral institution of the villages economy. The British policy of maximisation of revenue aggravated the inherited bankruptcy of the peasantry. Both N.N. Benarjee and S.L. Maddox admit the existence of extensive indebtedness of peasants in Orissa in the 19th century. Banerjee estimated that very nearly 75% of the agricultural population were in debt. The average peasant possessing 10 manas of land with five family members found himself perpetually in debt. Kindsford the revenue officer of Balasore, calculated that, the average income of such a peasant from cultivation was Rs. 41-10-6 but his annual expenditure was Rs. 46-10-6.[78] So, they mainly depended on money-lenders, mahajans, sahukars and banias. There were mainly two kinds of money-lenders. The first group of money-lenders were mainly controlling the commodity market and receiving payment of loan annually after the harvesting season in produce and thereby had a control over the grain export from the village and had contact with the mahajans of the towns.

There was another class of professional money-lenders who were a minority. They were sometimes without any agricultural pursuits and were called mahajans, sahukars or banias.[79] They figured prominently in the literary works of the contemporary writers like Fakir Mohan Senapati and Chintamani Mohanty.[80] Some of them were Kabulis, Marwaris, Gossain, Punjabi and Mohammadan who initially came to the village as blanket, textile and other commodity dealers, lent money during the off season at usurious rate of interest to collect during the harvesting reason.[81]

These money-lenders exploited the people in various ways. They were variously described by the contemporary civil servants of the British Raj. To J.B. Phear, the money-lender remained so involved in financing agricultural production that, they reduced the cultivator to the status of feudal labourer barely earning his livelihood.[82] Another modern historian M.J.K. Thavaraj described" the money-lenders of the nineteenth century in rural areas were the financial octopus.[83]

As a result, the migration of population became a conspicuous feature of Orissa during the period under review. Rapid growth of population, frequent natural calamities leading to crop failure and indebtedness, maximisation of revenue, large scale unemployment after the decline of salt and cottage industries led large number of people to proceed towards Rangoon, Assam and Calcutta as labourers. From the above analysis it is clear that agriculture was the chief occupation of the overwhelming majority of the people of Orissa. Trade was carried on an extremely limited scale. Very small number of the local people participated in trade. Only 1.5 percent of the total population were engaged in trade.[84] The major portion of it was controlled by the outsider. The Marwaris, Gujaratis and Bengalis who come to Orissa as traders, established their wholesale trade of consumer goods from Calcutta,[85] Bombay, Raipur and Nagpur. But they refrained from capital investment to industrialise Orissa during the period under review mainly due to lack of communication and paucity of mining explorations.[86]

The people of Orissa in general were also too unenterprising to take any part in trade beyond the passive one of sitting in their houses and selling their surplus produce to the Bengalis, Marwaris and merchants of Bombay who went to them. They would not easily go to different places to sell their produce at still higher prices.[87]

The people of Orissa did not receive proper attention of the British administration. Most of the officers were unable to understand the economic problems of Orissa. Most of the regions of Orissa remained in inaccessible forests. When the British officers could not reach the villages they had to depend solely in the opinion of the subordinate officers who were also ignorant about the economic system of the people. This was one of the vital reasons why many of the economic problems concerning industry, trade and commerce could not be examined by competent authorities which retarded the economic prosperity of the state.

Coupled with all these factors trade continued to be backward in Orissa during the period taken up for study. This was one of the principal causes of the abysmal poverty of the people of Orissa.

REFERENCES

1. T. Ray Choudhury and Irfan Habib (ed), The Cambridge economic history of India, Vol. I, p. 325.
2. J.N. Sarker, Mughal economy organisation and working, 1963, p.141.
3. Report on the administration of Bengal for the year 1883-84, Calcutta, 1884, p.14.
4. Annual general administration report of Orissa division, 1874-75, Calcutta. 1875, p.5.
5. Early european travellers in the Nagpur territories, Nagpur, 1930, p.156.
6. Bengal Judicial (Civil) proceedings, No.26, 5 Sept. 1805, Secy. to commissioner of Cuttack.
7. Maddox Report Vol. II.
8. Utkal Dipika, 24 May, 1873.
9. Maddox Report, Vol.1, p.421.
10. W.W. Hunter, History of Orissa, Vol.II, London, 1872, p.74.
11. Annual general administration report of Orissa division for the year 1889-90. p.57.
12. Final report on the settlement of Dhenkanal Feudatory State, 1923-24, Vol. I, p.6.
13. Maddox Report, Vol.II, p.468.
14. Early european travellers in Nagpur territories, Nagpur, 1930, p. 22.
15. Settlement report of Talcher State, 1911-12, p. 10.
16. Report on the administration of Bengal 1883-84, p. 14.
17. S.L. Maddox, Final report of the Survey and settlement of the province of Orissa, 1890 to 1900 A.D., Vol.I, p.7.
18. N. Senapati (ed), Orissa District Gazetteers, Sambalpur, Cuttack, 1971, p. 273.
19. Final report on the settlement of Dhenkanal Feudatory States, 1923-29, Vol.I, p.6.

20. W. W. Hunter, Statistical account of Bengal, Vol. XIX, London, 1877, pp. 263-64.
21. R.C.S. Bell, Op. Cit, p.122.
22. P.T. Mansfield, Bihar and Orissa District Gazetteers, Puri, 1929, pp. 221-222.
23. Orissa District Gazetteers, Cuttack, 1995, p.431.
24. Early european travellers in Nagpur territories, p.16.
25. W.W. Hunter, History of Orissa, Vol.II, London, 1872, p.65.
26. N.C. Behuria, Orissa District Gazetteers, Ganjam, pp. 410-411.
27. N.Senapati(ed), Orissa District Gazetteers, Sambalpur, Cuttack, 1971, p. 273.
28. N.C. Behuria (ed) Orissa District Gazetteers, Ganjam, Cuttack 1995, p. 409.
29. N. Senapati (ed), O.D.S. Puri-Cuttack, 1977, pp. 254-255.
30. Ibid, p. 255.
31. N. Senapati (ed), Orissa District Gazetter, Sambalpur, p. 275.
32. Ibid, p. 237.
33. N.C. Behuria, Orissa District Gazetteer, Ganjam, p. 410.
34. Bengal revenue proceedings mill's minute Tributary Mahals, 23 January, 1842.
35. Settlement of Kanika, p. 15, Settlement of Darpan, p. 16.
36. P. Mukherjee, History of Orissa, 1904, p. 179.
37. N. C. Behuria, Orissa District Gazetteer, Cuttack, 1996, p. 381.
38. Maddox Report, p. 29.
39. N. Senapati, Orissa District Gazetteer, Cuttack, 1977, p. 254.
40. Ibid.
41. N.C. Behuria, Orissa District Gazetteer, Cuttack, pp. 381-382.

42. Records of the Board of Revenue, R. Ker, Magistrate, Cuttack to Board of Revenue, Nov. 1. 1806, Orissa State Archieves.
43. N. C. Behuria, Orissa District Gazetteer, Cuttack, pp. 382-385.
44. General administration report of Orissa division, 1899-1900, p.31.
45. Ibid, p.8.
46. N. Senapati, Orissa District Gazetteer, Puri, pp. 257-258.
47. Administrative report of Orissa, 1873-74, p. 10.
48. Ibid, 1883-84, p.10.
49. B. C. Ray, Foundations of British in Orissa, 1960, p. 187.
50. C. R., Wilson, Early annals of the english in Bengal Vol.II, Part-I, No.1014.
51. Madala Panji, p. 67.
52. Dairies of Streynsham Master, Vol.II, pp. 45-48.
53. N. Senapati, Orissa District Gazetteer, Puri, p. 251.
54. Letter of Sherer, Accountant General to Government of Bengal, Revenue Consultations, 24.10.1817, No. 42.
55. B. C. Ray, Foundations of British Orissa, 1960, pp. 189-190.
56. Harcourt to Mr. Shaw. Private Secretary to Governor General, August 9, 1804, also quoted B.C. Ray Foundations of British Orissa, p. 190.
57. Letter of Richardson to Government on 8.1.1814 Bengal Revenue Consultations.
58. B. C. Ray Foundations of British Orissa, 1960, p. 203.
59. Letter of Ewer to Government of Bengal, Bengal Revenue Consultations, No. 15.
60. P. Mukherjee, History of Orissa, 1904, pp. 467-68.
61. N. C. Behuria, Orissa District Gazetteer, Ganjam,

Cuttack, 1995, p. 378.
62. N. Senapati (ed), Orissa District Gazetteer, Sambalpur, 1971, p. 249.
63. N. C. Behuria, Orissa District Gazetteer, Ganjam, p. 378.
64. N. Senapati, (ed), Orissa District Gazetteer, Puri, p. 262.
65. N. Senapati Orissa District Gazetteer, Sambalpur, p. 245.
66. Ibid, p. 245.
67. Utkal Dipika, 18.8.1866.
68. L.S.S.O.' Malley, Bengal District Gazetteer, Balasore, Calcutta, 1907, pp. 84-85.
69. N. K. Jit, "The Agrarian life and economy of Orissa (1833-1897) Calcutta, 1884, p. 84.
70. Maddox Report, Vol.I, Calcutta, 1900, p. 119.
71. Utkal Dipika, 19.2.1881.
72. Maddox Report, Vol.I, Calcutta, 1900, p. 121.
73. R. C. S. Bell, Orissa District Gazetteer, Koraput, Cuttack, 1945, p.121.
74. Ibid, p. 121.
75. T. Motte, Early europeans travellers in Nagpur territories, p. 16.
76. Settlement report of Talcher State, 1911-12, p. 10.
77. R.C.S Bell, Op. Cit, p. 121-122.
78. Maddox Report, Vol. I, pp. 249-256.
79. Gangadhar Granthabali, Cuttack, 1972, p. 344.
80. Fakir Mohan Senapati, Atma Jivani Charitra, Cuttack, 1963, p. 19.
81. Report of bengal provincial banking inquiry committee, 1928-30, Calcutta, 1930, p. 58.
82. J. B. Pheare, Indian famine and village organisation, London, 1872, p. 12.
83. M.J.K. Thavaraj, Framework of economic policies under British rule, Journal of peasant studies, No. 77 Dec. 1978, pp. 24-25.

84. N. C. Behuria, Orissa District Gezetteer Ganjam, p.371.
85. F. M. Senapati, Fakir Mohan Granthavali, Part-I, Cuttack, 1963, p. 187.
86. India Industrial Commission, Minutes of guidances 1916-17, Vol. II, Calcutta 1918, p. 770.
87. General administration report of Orissa division, 1874-75, p.5.

Chapter - 4

OVERSEAS TRADE

Being situated on the shore of the Bay of Bengal, Orissa had all the privileges of developing ports and conducting overseas trade with a number of countries since time immemoral.[1] Orissa, famous as Kalinga in ancient times had a long maritime history. During the days of yore, the people of Kalinga were the pioneers of conducting extensive maritime trade with foreign countries like Sumatra, Java, Borneo, Malayan Peninsula, Annam, China, Combodia, East Indies, Siam, Brahmadesh (Burma), Simhala and the islands of the pacific from the famous ports at Kalingapattanam, Palur, Chitrotpala, Tamralipti and Charitra.[2]

The Buddhist literature Si-yu-ki, Jatakas, Dattadhatuvamsa and Lalitavistara record the existence of a number of ports in ancient Orissa. Ptolemy has also given a very interesting description of the ports of Orissa Kautilya in his 'Arthasastra' renders a very bright description of shipping activities of Orissa and its administrative look out in the department of trade and commerce. Gunadhya's 'Baddkaha', Somadeva's 'Kathasarita Sagar' and Acharya Dandi's 'Dasakumara Charita' also record the ancient sea-voyages of the mariners or traders of Kalinga from the port of Tamralipti.[3] Kalidas, the celebrated poet of the 5th century India, in his 'Raghuvamsa' described the king of Kalinga as 'Mahadadhipati' which means the Lord of the Ocean. There was a time when the present Bay of Bengal was known as the Kalinga Sagar or the sea of Kalinga due to the predominance of the Oriya sailors and navigators over this port of the Indian Ocean.[4]

The story of the pilgrimage of Danta Kumar and Hemamala from Dantapur in Kalinga to the island of Simhala, the description of the sea voyages from the ports of Tamralipti and Cheletalo to Simhala, China and other places as given by the famous chinese pilgrim Hiuen-Tsang in 645 A.D. and the ceremonial taking of the original manuscript "Ganda Vyuha" by the celebrated Buddhist Scholar Prajna from the king of Udra to the chinese emperor on sea-voyage in 794 A.D. bear ample testimony to the maritime activities of the people of Kalinga in ancient times.[5]

Orissa's cultural and political relations with the countries of south-east Asia form a fascinating chapter in the history of Orissa. At first because of commercial reasons, the Orissan sailors reached these places. Subsequently, political and cultural ties strengthened the relations. It appears that, voyages from the ports of Kalinga to the islands of south-east Asia were fairly common. Legends of Java relate that "20,000 families were sent to Java by the prince of Kalinga (Kaling)." These people prospered and multiplied. Chinese sources of Tang period reveals that, a new name Ho-ling was given to a town of Java. Scholars generally agree that, Ho-ling is a Chinese form of Kalinga. The presence of a state in Java bearing the name

Ho-ling (Kalinga) obviously suggests that, the region was dominated by the people from Kalinga. There are indications to believe that the celebrated Sailendra dynasty-the immortal builders of Borobudder in Java are said to have been the descendants of the Sailodbhava dynasty of Orissa.[6]

These historic facts are further corroborated by the numerous stone carvings depicting shipping activities seen to-day in the facades of the Konark, Bhahmeswar and Jagannath temples and other literary evidences in this country. The traces of Kalingan architecture in the monuments of the far-east speak of our ancient heritage. A sculptured frieze collected from the vicinity of the Brahmaswara temple in Bhubaneswar depicts boats carrying elephants. An interesting sculpture of Orissa, supposed to have been collected from Konark and now preserved in the Indian Museum, Calcutta, depicts a boat being rowed by four persons and a royal personage sits inside the boat. There is also an elephant in the boat. The sculptured panel of the Konark temple shows the king being presented with a giraffe. The giraffe is purely an African animal and its presence is an important evidence of Orissa's commercial contact with east Africa.[7]

This glorious maritime tradition of Orissa is preserved in a unique manner, being intimately linked with some of the religious practices and festivals of Orissa. On Kartika purnima day, colourful paper boats are floated on tanks and rivers. This has became an annual ritual reminding us of the hundreds of merchants who used to set sail on the ocean to seek wealth by commerce.[8] The glory and prosperity of ancient Orissa was probably due to her foreign trade and commerce with the distant lands.[9]

Thus, ancient and medieval Orissa played a leading role in the overseas trade in India. But by the middle of the 16th century A.D., the maritime trade of Orissa had dwindled due to a number of reasons. First, the decline and fall of the Orissan kingdom adversely affected the volume of maritime trade in Orissa. From the year 1568 A.D. Orissa suffered from the political rule of the Afghans Mughals, Marathas and then the British through successive ages. This political subjugation became a formidable barrier to the merchants and trading communities of Orissa. In the 17th century Orissa's sea-borne trade passed into the hands of the european merchants as they enjoyed the patronage of the Muslim rulers. The wealth and opulence of the province as well as the rich variety of manufactured goods allured the British to establish their factories at Hariharpur (1633), Balasore (1633) and at Pipli (1634). Not only the English but also the French, the Danes, the Dutch and the portuguese established their factories about the middle of the 17th century in Orissa.[10] But at that time, the manufacture and trade of Orissa were very inconsiderable and unimportant. The English made efforts to establish trade settlements from the second decade of the 17th century. The draft treaty concluded between Jahangir and Sir Thomas Roe in 1616 mentioned that the English "Shall come freely to any port in the territory of the said king of India as well in Bangla and Syndu (sind) as in the lordship of Surat".[11]

Under the patronage of the Marathas, salt and cloth were important articles to be exported in plenty. The ports of Harishpur, Pipli and Balasore prospered and these places were the centres of commercial activities, full of din and bustle. Ship building centres were found at Balasore and there was a profitable brisk trade patronised by the Maratha government. Thus, trade and commerce was beneficial and prosperous on the eve of the British conquest of Orissa.[12]

But due to the monopolistic attitude of the British merchants, the commercial prosperity of the province had gradually dwindled by the end of the 18th century.

Two European travellers, Tomas Motte and Leckie, who passed through Orissa in the second half of the 18th century did not find its maritime commercial prosperity at all. Leckie in his account stated that "Balasore was formerly a flourishing port, but their manufacture of Sanoes cloth is very much fallen off, both in quality and quantity and the ruinous state of the English and Dutch factories with the insignificance of the Danish one, seem to show that the trade is not of that consequence which it formerly was.[13] No further information is available from his accounts about the trade and commerce of Orissa.

However, when the British occupied Orissa in 1803, they took some steps to rebuild the ports and revive the sea-borne trade of Orissa.[14] Their interest in trade and industry led to the discovery and opening of ports like Dhamrah, Churaman, Chhanua, Sartha, Subarnarekha and Lochanpur in Balasore district and Puri, Davee, Sahandhu & Matta in the Puri district, Ganjam and Gopalpur in the Ganjam district.

All the ports that were there, were of little use when exposed to the ordeal of bad weather or any other emergency. Even then they were largely used by the foreign and indian merchants to carry on export and import trade. The maximum volume of trade passed through the principal ports at Balasore and Gopalpur. The main articles of export were rice and paddy. The quantity exported depended on the state of crops in Orissa and the demand for it in the neighbouring provinces.

Gradually the decline was perceptible in the export of cotton goods. Large quantities of cloth were being imported from Europe and sold at a cheaper rate in the Orissa market. The people generally preferred cheap foreign goods to costly indigenous products. Andrew Stirling wrote in 1825, "The manufactures and trade of Orissa proper are very inconsiderable and unimportant". A sufficiency of the coarser clothes is made for the use of the inhabitants of all parts of the district. The calicoes of Balasore, Sore, Bhadrak, Janjipur (Jajpur) and Hariharpur were once much prized and sought after under the name of sanoes, but the demand for the finer fabrics of that description have long since greatly declined; the quantity now manufactured is very trifling.[15]

PORTS OF ORISSA ON THE EVE OF THE FAMINE OF 1866

By the time the famine broke out there was no port of any significance in Orissa. All the ports that were there, were of little use when exposed to the ordeal of bad weather or any emergency. Orissa had no good system of communication. Hence it was generally inaccessible to the ordinary course of trade and was often found to have been cut off from the outside world.[16]

In 1866 Orissa did not have a single harbour, capable of sheltering ship of any size. No port offered a secured anchorage during the monsoon. In the same season ships or steamers could not land cargoes on its surfbeaten shore. Further, great difficulty was experienced in loading and unloading ships and steamers. Due to the absence of good harbours, rice could not be imported into Orissa on a large scale to meet the needs of the famine-stricken people. Even then, after 1866 the British authorities did not bother seriously about the development of ports.

False-point was the most important of the Orissa ports in 1866. The famine commission of 1866 considered it to be the best harbours on the whole coast of India between Hooghly and Bombay. It was situated at the mouth of the river Mahanadi, at a distance of 70 miles from the town of Cuttack. The port had been discovered and opened in 1860 and it was expected to provide protected anchorage. An agency had been established there for the export of rice. But there was no means of disembarking the cargo and passengers at the anchorage. There was also no good communication between the port and the interior parts of the country.

The Balasore port was situated on the river Burabalanga. In the 17th century it was the seat of considerable trade. Eventually it became much less useful by the formation of sand across the mouth of the river. The Puri port was nominally a port, because it was very shallow and steamers could not approach it within a distance of some miles.[17]

In spite of the absence of good harbours, the export trade of Orissa was considerable and averaged 20,000 tonnes of rice a year during the six years preceeding 1865. The price of rice had generally remained cheap as compared with other provinces. Though they themselves had not undertaken any large mercantile operations, their surplus grain had been sought by others for this reasons. The surplus from the crop of 1864 has been carried off "by the energetic Telingah, Kumutis of Madras territory who have secured the country to by up the grain and an enterprising french house (Messrs Robert Cherriol and Company) who have exported largely by way of false-point". The quantity exported was unusually large, viz. 33,000 tonnes of which Balasore alone sent away 26,000 tonnes. Despite the general panic in 1865-66, 70,727 mounds had been exported from the province by the end of October 1866. The unusual brisk exportation decreased the stocks to a considerable extent and contributed to the Orissa famine of 1866.[18]

Adhering strictly to the policy of laissez-faire, the British authorities did not import rice well in time to meet the needs of the famine-stricken people. When the famine reached gigantic proportion and starvation became more and more general in June 1866, they had no other option but to order the immediate importation of rice into Orissa. But the importation was very much obstructed due to the outburst of monsoon on the Orissa coast with terrific violence. Not much rice could be shipped as there was no good harbours on the Orissa coast. Another difficulty was, when the ships had brought rice to the coast, to get the rice unloaded and carry up to the interior when the ship had brought it to the coast. It was not till September that any sufficient quantity of rice had reached the centres of demand. June, July and August were the months in which famine was intensely felt.[19] It left one million people of Cuttack, Puri and Balasore districts dead. The timely importation of grain would have been of real help in averting the horrors of the famine.

Ports of Orissa After 1866

Owing to the change in the course of rivers, shifting of the sea and silting of the river mouths, some of the ports had ceased to exist while the position of others had been changed. The ports that existed were not very useful from the commercial point of view. In 1873, John Beams, the collector of Balasore observed : "A stranger coming by sea to Balasore on seeing our harbours would think he had arrived at the dominions of some independent native chief who did not know what were the requirements of the civilized countries in respect of portal accommodation. He would be subject to the greatest maritime power, the world had ever seen."[20]

The famine commission of 1866 dwelt on the necessity of improvement of communication both by land and sea with a view to preventing the recurrence of similar disaster. It pressed the necessity of improvement of the port of Orissa so as to accommodate ocean-going vessels. It drew the attention of the government to the existing defects of the ports and suggested for their development.

The false-point was the only port which received some attention of the government after the famine. It was surveyed and deepened and the channels were buoyed. Although the government effected some improvement of the false-point, the plan was abandoned subsequently. Formerly no vessel approached the coast due to summer monsoon and after the improvements had been affected the port remained open throughout the year.[21]

As late as 1866, the false-point at the mouth of the river Mahanadi was largely used. but unfortunately, the sea receded there towards the east. In rough weather, steamers could not go near the false-point. They had to anchor for a very considerable distance as it was impossible, for the steamers to load and unload their contents there. Owing to difficulties of loading a major portion of trade of this port was diverted towards Chandabali and coast canal. S.L. Maddox stated that for all practical and commercial purposes, the port lost much of its utility by the end of the 19th century.[22]

The ports of Balasore district which received the attention of the goverment after the famine were (1) Balasore (2) Dhamra (3) Churaman (4) Sartha (5) Suvarnarekha and (6) Lychanpur. Balasore was situated on the river Boorabalanga, 16 miles from the coast. In the 19th century it was a seat of considerable trade and eventually trade was stopped by the formation of a sand bar across the mouth of the river. This flourishing port was discovered by the Britishers when they entered into the city in 1803 and found the port in a dilapidated condition. However, this port was declared as a port of Orissa in 1858. No permanent improvement of the port of Balasore was undertaken. Nothing concrete was done to develop this port as it involved great engineering difficulties and large outlay. The government spent a very small sum in buoying channels and dredging sand bars. The opening of coast canal to traffic in 1887 not only further facilitated the silting of Balasore port at the mouth of the Burabalanga river but also diverted large portion of the seaborne trade of the district through it.[23]

The new port of Chandabali or Ravensport was opened in 1872.[24] It was situated on the Balasore side of the river 25 miles from the coast. It was an inland port on the river Baitarani, a river running between the district of Cuttack and Balasore. It was accessible by tidal creak, 25 miles to the north and 70 miles to the south.[25] Captain Macneil discovered the adaptability of Chandabali port for the passenger traffic, free from all risks of inundation and having sufficient depth of water. During the whole period of famine this port had helped the government in respect of the import of foodgrains to Balasore and Cuttack districts when this port was growing rapidly on the whole of the coast, a storm passed over the port on September 22, 1885 devastating it.[26] After the initiative of the government, Chandabali port was improved and light steamers ran almost daily to and from Calcutta and this Chandabali port became an important place for coastal trade.[27]

Dhamra guarded the estuary which had been formed at the mouth of Baitarani and Brahmani rivers. It included the navigable channels of all the rivers as far as they were affected by the tidal waters.[28] There was a custom house and one pilot house to give shelter to pilots of the vessels coming to the port.[29] Dhamra continued to serve as a port of Orissa upto 1894.

The Subarnarekha was situated in the month of river, Subarnarekha. After the decline of the

Pipli port, the europeans shifted their centre of activities to this port. Sartha was situated at the junction of two rivers Panchapara and Sartha which flowed into the Bay of Bengal, a few miles below Subarnarekha. Due to the silting of rivers this port became unsuitable for accommodating vessels. Hence, the government paid no attention to improve this port but it was declared as a port of Orissa in the year 1858.[30] Panchapara had taken the place of Sartha port in the course of time.

Churaman was an open road stead in the mouth of Gummere river, a branch of Kansbas. This port was included in the list of ports according to the provisions of Act 11 of 1858. But the port fell into disuse by the deposits of silt and mud.[31] Lychanpore was not far away on a small creek of the river Lychanpore. It played an important role in the growth of sea-borne trade in Balasore district as well as in Orissa. Gradually it ceased to exist in Orissa as government did not like to spend money on this port.

The ports of Puri district opened in 1860 also drew attention of the government after the famine. They were six in number-Puri, Davee, Sahandu, Mettacooah, Futtypore and Nundla.[32] The ports were in better position but due to lack of proper maintenance and supervision, these ports were turned simply to be road-stead. Puri remained behind other districts in respect of ports.

The ports of Orissa, however, were not paid the attention which they deserved. Adequate attention was not paid to the port of false-point. The harbour scheme and the establishment of a port town and location was much talked about, written about, planned, surveyed and estimated, the subject advanced a stage but no definite action was taken.[33] But famine in Bengal and consequently the financial difficulties prevented the government from proper allotment of funds to port improvements.[34] Similarly no permanent improvement of the port Subarnarekha was undertaken as it would involve great engineering difficulties and cost. Further, the dense jungles on the bank of the river afforded great opportunities for smuggling which was found difficult to check without expensive establishment.[35] The tendency of Balasore rivers to silt at the mouth had been fatal to the stability of every port in the district.[36]

After the famine of Orissa in 1866, the famine commission made specific recommendations for the development of ports in Orissa for communication purposes.[37] Finding the brisk activities of ports the Lt. Governor of Bengal sanctioned the following sums of money for the development of the following ports.

False-point	Rs.	2,89,000/-
Balasore	Rs.	30,000/-
Dhamra & Chandabali	Rs.	1,00,000/-
Puri	Rs.	20,000/-

But due to famine and disinterest of the British officials, funds were not properly allotted.[38] The development of ports of Orissa did not receive necessary attention to the British authorities for the following reasons. Firstly, the famines in Bengal presidency and Madras presidency and consequent financial difficulties prevented them from allotting required funds to port improvements.

Secondly, the construction of the coast canal in 1885 facilitated the silting of Balasore rivers and provided a new waterway and diverted a portion of sea-borne trade of the district. Thirdly, the extension of railway system through Orissa during 1890's further contributed to the decline of sea-borne trade. Balasore port was not in demand after the opening of the railways.[39] Besides the absence of the industrial and commercial enterprises of the Oriyas might have been a subsidiary factor for which the government remained indifferent to the development of ports to make them "independent and profit yielding."

Export and Import Trade

The opening of the port of false-point in 1860 and Chandabali port in 1870 together with the improved means of communication gave impetus to the maritime trade after 1866. From the ports of Orissa like False-point, Chandabali, Puri and Gopalpur, Stemers and sailing vessels plied to the coast of Burma, Madras and Bengal as well as to Ceylone, the Laccadive and Maldive Islands and Mauritious. Plenty of rice was exported to Madras port, Ceylone, Maldive island, and Mauritious. The imports were chiefly made from Calcutta, Bombay and Madras ports.[40]

The canal system was developed in Orissa after 1866. By 1898, there were 205 miles of canals available both for irrigation and navigation. These canals were very useful in carrying export trade. The coast canal which connected the Hooghly at Geonkhali with the river Matai at Charabatia was largely used by the merchants for the exportation of rice through the ports of False-point, Chandabali and Calcutta. The Kendrapara and Goberi extension canals connected Cuttack with the Brahmani at Alba, and from there boats went down the river to Chandabali, where cargo was transhipped and carried by steamers to Calcutta. The Taladanda canal between the Mahanadi and the Kathjuri rivers connected Cuttack with false-point, from which rice was shipped chiefly to the Mauritious. The high level canal supplied a direct route between the marts of Cuttack and Bhadrak.[41]

American, British and French ships visited five important ports, i.e. False-point, Puri, Balasore, Chandabali and Gopalpur at regular intervals. The vessels of British India Steam Navigation and Co. Ltd., the Scindia Steam Navigation and Co. Ltd. and the Asiatic Navigation and Co. Ltd. were engaged in carrying on export and import trade with these ports. The vessels of the first two companies had regular services between Gopalpur and Rangoon for cargo and passengers. A regular service for carrying cargoes and passengers was kept up between Chandabali and Calcutta by the Bengal and Orissa Steamship Company and the Chandabali Steamship Service Company.[42]

A considerable quantity of grain exported came from the Garhjats and several traders from Balasore visited princely states of Nilgiri and Mayurbhanj and purchased the crops upon the fields. At Chandabali also, it was a common practice for the exporters to send out agents among the villages, who purchased the crops before they were reaped by making advances to the cultivators. Rice was shipped overseas to Ceylone and Mauritious and sugar was obtained from the later island by merchants who kept up a connection with mohamadan traders controlling the sugar industry there. But with these exceptions trade, both import and export, was carried on chiefly with Calcutta and Madras.[43]

A regular service for carrying cargoes and passengers was kept up between Chandabali and Calcutta by the Bengal and Orissa Steamship Company and the Chandabali Steamship Service Company. With the opening of the railways, passengers ceased to use this route to Calcutta. But Chandabali continued to be the only port by which export and import trade of north Orissa was carried on.[44]

The main articles of export were foodgrains, agricultural and forest products and the imported articles in all the ports of Orissa were metal, gunny bags, kerosene oil, sugar, tobacco, lead, copper, zinc, glassware, liquors, spices, gold, silver and other machine-made fancy goods including cloth. The heavy burden caused by the imported articles was to be entirely shouldered by the only important item of export of rice. The imports were chiefly made from Calcutta, Bombay and Madras. With the development of both inland and overseas communications, there was great increase in the level of business activity in the province and there was a rapid increase in sea-borne trade.

From 1868-69 the business activity of the ports of Orissa was constantly on the increase. The number of vessels visiting different ports gradually increased. The number of vessels visited Balasore port were 232 in 1869-70, 277 in 1870-71, 275 in 1871-72, 345 in 1872-73, 405 in 1873-74 and 387 in 1874-75. The tonnage of vessels visiting the Puri port was 10,533 in 1874-

75.[45] as against 147 in 1867-68 and 1356 in 1868-69. The tonnage of vessels during 1874-75 was 51,689 as against 15,456 in 1869-70.[46] A similar increase was also found at false-point in Cuttack. The number of vessels visiting the port in 1868-69 was 15 as against 179 in 1878-79 and the tonnage of the vessels in 1868-69 was 13,574 as against 1,38,679 in 1878-79.[47]

For study of growth of trade of the province we might look closely into the trade statistics, the value of trade of the ports of Orissa. The following table shows the growth of sea-borne trade from 1868-69 to 1878-79.

Year	***Value of Imports in Rs.***	***Value of Export in Rs.***
1868-69	369486.00	269545.00
1869-70	715632.00	777034.00
1870-71	1356087.00	1336755.00
1871-72	1588000.00	1211411.00
1872-73	1174994.00	1416170.00
1873-74	2091288.00	3007175.00
1874-75	3592857.00	4391035.00
1875-76	3473774.00	3270714.00
1876-77	4725117.00	7661260.00
1877-78	9055184.00	10101291.00
1878-79	5640953.00	8148501.00
1881-82	6690026.00	6842784.00
1882-83	5496242.00	7704748.00
1883-84	7495108.00	8587718.00
1884-85	9115021.00	9653531.00
1885-86	8814173.00	9206142.00
1886-87	7619699.00	7631225.00[48]

It will appear from these figures that there was a rapid increase in the value of trade at Orissa port. The figures in the intermediate years notwithstanding the fluctuations revealed, to show a steady development.

But during the nineties, the figures notwithstanding fluctuations revealed a tendency towards decline.

Year	***Total Value of Trade in Rs.***
1887-88	14045584.00
1888-89	11328986.00
1890-91	16115263.00
1893-94	11459770.00
1894-95	11973792.00
1899-1900	12075438.00
1900-1901	8748465.00
1901-1902	8207848.00[49]

From the year 1887, the maritime trade of north, Orissa showed a tendency towards decline. The coast canal absorbed a large portion of the external trade of north Orissa by providing a new waterways. With the abandonment of salt manufacture in Cuttack, Puri and Balasore district, the export received further setback. The extension of railways to Orissa contributed much to the decline of portal trade. The deteriorating condition of ports of Orissa, the callousness of the government to improve the ports of Orissa, the heavy rate of duty on the articles of export and import and the abandonment of salt manufacture accelerated the process of decline of the sea trade in Orissa towards the end of the 19th century. As a result of which the economic conditions of the province naturally declined.

In Orissa, the rise in exports was closely followed by the rise in imports. A closer examination of the figures brings out the additional fact that the increase in imports kept pace with the rise in exports throughout the period which was very different from all India trend during the period. In 1873-74 and 1874-75, the export trade of Orissa received a boost owing to sudden demand for rice on account of famine in Bengal. Consequently there was a rise in the value of exports which was followed by a rise in the value of imports. Throughout the later period also the rise in imports kept pace with the rise in exports. The conclusion from the above statement comes to the point that the export surplus or what was called the *drain of wealth to England* was not remarkable in Orissa as in was general in India.[50]

Impact of maritime trade on Orissa's economy

Maritime trade of Orissa under the British rule adversely affected the economy of Orissa. It proved to be more harmful than helpful. It contributed to the impoverishment of peasants and artisan classes. It was one of the major causes of the famines and scarcities that occurred during the British rule.

In course of time markets of Orissa were flooded with machine-made goods which were obviously of superior quality and sold at a cheaper rate. The collapse of the rural artisan industries was caused largely by competition with the cheaper imported machine goods from England. The cotton weaving and spinning industries were worst hit. The export trade of the province during 19th century consisted mainly of food stuffs and other agricultural products, skin and hides, oil seeds, jutes, timbers, jungle products, such as lac, wax, tusser, feather, coconuts, and dried fish and its imports consisted in manufacturers such as cotton piece goods, salt, gunny bags, kerosene oil, sugar, glassware, liquors, spices, fancy goods, potatoes, tobacco and metals like lead, copper, zinc, gold and silver.

As regards the weaving industry as a whole, it might be said that the products of the local looms could not, at any rate in the towns and larger villages, compete with the machine, made articles of english manufacture, though some were prized for their fine texture. Even then hand-woven cotton cloths still held their own in rural tracts, owing to their durability. On the whole, the industry was not thriving and the weavers were taking up other means of earning their livelihood in increasing numbers.

Gopabandhu Das raised voice in order to improve the lot of the country weaver, blacksmith, goldsmith or the shoe-maker. He stated "It is needless to say that weaving has from time immemorial been the chief cottage industry in the country but most of the handloom weavers have under the peculiar economic pressure caused by foreign influences been driven out of their family occupation and are now reduced to extreme poverty. A movement organised for the revival of the industry will not only help a dying community but will foster a spirit for new industries among our artisan classes."[51]

The sale of the imported salt was increasing after 1863. By 1898 the salt industry in Orissa become almost extinct due to the unhealthy competition of liverpool and Madras salt. Consequently nearly 40,000 people of Balasore, Cuttack and Puri districts were deprived of their means of livelihood. Dislocation of any single community from its proper economic position affected other economic groups. Pandit Gopabandhu Das rightly observed:

"When I see the great body of labourers suffering year by year for want of employment and hopelessly leaving their wives and children, going out to Burma and Assam in quest of wages. I cannot but bewail the loss Orissa has sustained at the hands of officers who should have looked at the situation with sympathy, a liberal spirit and in a statesman like way.[52]

Most of the ruined handicraftsmen, artisans and salt-makers failed to find alternative employment. The only choice open to them was to depend upon agriculture. The increasing pressure on agriculture resulted in the steady deterioration in the material condition of the rural people.

Rice was the chief articles of export. The sea export of foodgrains from the province continued to rise. It amounted to 1,28,000 maunds in 1868-69, 3,00,000 maunds in 1869-70, 4,00,000 mounds in 1870-71, 4,83,000 maunds in 1871-72, 4,00,00 maunds in 1872-73, 12,84,881 maunds in 1873-74 and 17,54,645 maunds in 1876-77. It so happened that even at the time of scarcities, the export of food was as brisk as ever. Although in 1873-74 the crop was only an average one in Balasore, it exported about one million and a third of maunds of rice. In 1877-78, exportation was carried on to such a dangerous extent that there were unmistakable signs of exhaustion of surplus stock. Although Puri was the least important of the Orissa ports, its export of rice was too high.[53]

Several factors were responsible for the increasing exportation of rice from Orissa. Rice was cheaper here in comparison with other provinces of India. The deep poverty of the people compelled them to sell rice at a low price during the harvesting season. Besides, Orissa's long coastline had some ports affording people scope for carrying on export of rice.

With the increasing in export of rice, the price of rice showed a constant rise and rice became scarce. In 1865, the normal rate of rice was 30 to 40 seers per rupee. Whereas the average price of the rice between 1867 and 1876 was 26 seers per rupees, it was 21 seers between 1877-1886 and 18 seers between 1886-1898.[54]

The rise of price of rice caused great hardship to the labouring classes because their wages did not rise in the same proportion as the rise in prices. Whereas their daily wages was 2 annas in 1814, it was 3 annas in 1889.[55] The rise of price did not benefit small farmers as they did not have much to sell. Besides, most of them sold their produce either to money-lenders or to rice traders at a low rate during the harvesting seasons. Rise of price was a source of trouble for the shop-keepers and government employees. Actually big farmers and landlords reaped the benefit of high prices. Willium Hunter observed that even in normal years one-fifth of the total population of forty million people went through life on insufficient food. And the rise of prices was felt as a great hardship to the large population of shop-keepers and government employees in Cuttack town also.[56]

The merchants of Orissa did not gain much from the export and import trade. Oriyas had little commercial enterprise. They did not possess capital to engage directly in trade. Orissa's import and export trade was practically in the hands of outsiders. The rice merchants were principally Mohamandans from Bombay and Koomutees from Madras and the cloth merchants were Marwaries from Jeypore and Marwar and the hide dealers, Kabulies from Afghanisthan.[57] Besides several english firms like Messers Brett Brothers, Messers Chambers and Company and Messers Valetta and Company kept up their agencies in Cuttack, Puri and Chandabali to look after their commercial interests. There were hardly one or two Oriya merchants.

The social relevance of Orissan maritime activity was no less profound. With the rise of european settlements and the emergency of port-towns and urban centres, the coastal areas of Orissa soon fell under the evil influence of cosmopolitan life. Prostitution, slavery and drinking of wine became a fashion of life in the port towns and urban centres of Orissa.

But there is not denying the fact that the maritime trade of Orissa in the 19th century before the opening of railways conferred some benefits on the people of Orissa. Firstly, the increasingly import of consumer goods (machine-made articles) was indicating of improvement in the standard of living of the people. Secondly, people in general got salt and cloth of fine quality at a cheaper rate. Thirdly, the rising export trade in rice brought about improvement in the material condition of the big farmers by disposing their produce and reaped the benefit of high prices.

Fourthly, export of such minor items like hide, oil-seeds, coconut, fish, dried fish and jungle products yielded some profit to the people of Orissa who were supplying them. Lastly, the most far-reaching result was the demand of food-grains which led to the extension of cultivation. Owing to rising prices and increasing export of rice land was diverted from other crops to paddy, The rise in prices directly benefited the cultivating class who paid their rent in cash.

During the period under review several factors fostered maritime trade in Orissa. They were the improvement of the False-point, establishment of the Chandabali port, the opening of navigable canals and the development of road system. The principal export was rice and the largest imports were salt and european piece goods. The port of Orissa exported large quantities of rice to Madras ports, Ceylon, Mauritious, Laccadive and Maldive islands.

The continued silting of the sands at the rive mouths and almost total lack of proper care of the ports proved fatal to the functioning of the ports of Orissa. The ports of Orissa which were of any use were Puri, Chandabali and Gopalpur. The abandonment of salt manufacture was a great blow to the export trade of Orissa. The opening of the coast canal in 1887 and extension of the railway during the closing years of the 19th century facilitated the decline of the maritime trade of Orissa. After 1900 much of Orissa's export were sent to important cities and ports of India by railway communications. The railways had a paralysing effect on the entire sea borne trade of Orissa.

Maritime trade of Orissa was designed to serve the interests of British imperialism. The worst feature of maritime trade of British Orissa was that outside vessels had displaced Orissa's sea-going vessels and outside merchants (indian and foreign) had captured her trade. The influx of foreign goods and consequent destruction of the weaving and salt industries of Orissa, continuous export of rice from Orissa and consequent scarcity of foodgrains and handling of the maritime trade of Orissa by the outside merchants proved most harmful in their effects. The redeeming feature of the maritime trade was the displacement of indigenous products by machine-made articles, indicating a changing pattern of living, but the improvement of communication, rising export trade was certainly and indication of development which gave the province the advantage of security against another famine by facilitating mobility of labour and importation of foodgrains.

REFERENCES

1. R.D. Banerjee, History of Orissa, Vol. I, 1936, p. 94.
2. Ibid, p. 98. It throws some light as the people of Kalinga taking part in colonising these islands.
3. Maritime activities and trade in Orissa. Orissa state archieves, Bhubaneswar, 1996, p. 4.
4. K. S. Behera, Maritime trade in ancient Orissa, Cuttack, p. 115.
5. R. C. Majumdar, Hindu colonies in Far-Fast, Calcutta, 1994, p. 19.
6. R. C. Majumdar, Ancient indian colonies in the Far-East, Vol. II, Calcutta, 1994, p. 227.
7. M. N. Das (ed) Side lights on history and culture of Orissa, Cuttack, 1977, p. 115.
8. K S. Behera, op. cit, p. 114.
9. B. C. Ray, Orissa under the Mughals, 1981, p. 138.
10. Proceedings of the Indian history congress, 14th session, Jaipur, "Shipping and maritime activities of Orissa during the Muslim rule", pp. 172-176.
11. Sir, Thomas Roe (1615-1619) "The Embassy of Sir Thomas Roe to the court of the great Mogols", (ed.) by Sir William Foster, Hakluyt society, 1899, p. 134.
12. B. C. Ray, New lights of Marathas Orissa, 1993, p. 226.
13. Early European travellers in the Nagpur territories Nagpur, 1930, p. 521.
14. G. Toynbee, A sketch of the history of Orissa

(1803-1828) Calcutta, 1873, p. 88.

15. A Stirling, An account of Orissa proper of Cuttack, London, 1846, p. 21.
16. G. C. Pattanaik, The famine and some aspects of the British economic policy in Orissa (1866-1909), 1980, p. 176.
17. S. L. Maddox, Final report on the survey and settlement of the province of Orissa, 1890 to 1900, Vol. I, p. 10.
18. Report of the commissioners appointed to enquire into the famine in Bengal and Orissa, 1866, Vol. I, Para-47.
19. Report of the Indian famine commission, 1880, Part-I, p. 43.
20. Quoted in the report on the administration of the Customs department, Govt. of Bengal, 1874-75, p. 176.
21. H. L. Dampier, Secy., Govt. of Bengal to Secy., Govt. of India, No. 3345, 22 October 1868, Utkal Dipika, Part-IV, 3 July, 1869, No. 27.
22. S. L. Maddox, Final report on the survey and settlement of the province of Orissa, 1890 to 1900 Vol. I, p. 10.
23. Ibid, p. 43.
24. W. W. Hunter, History of Orissa, London, 1872, p. 88.
25. H. L. Dampier, Secy., Govt. of Bengal to Secy., Govt. of India., No. 3345, 22 October 1868., Bengal Revenue Proc. Nov. 1868, Utkal Dipika, Part-IV, 3 July, 1869, No. 27.
26. C. E. Buckland Bengal under Lt. Governor, Vol. II, 1902, p. 822.

27. General administration report of Orissa division, 1873-74, p. 10.
28. Balasore Custom house reports, 1842.
29. File No. 159/1894, Board of Revenue, Commissioner of Customs to Board of Revenue, No. 948, September 24, 1894.
30. Maddox Report, p. 43.
31. Bengal revenue proceedings, November, 1875.
32. H. L. Dampier, Secy., Govt. of Bengal to Secy. Govt. of India, No. 3345, 22 October, 1868, Bengal revenue proceedings, Nov. 1868.
33. G. C. Pattanaik, The famine and some aspects of the British economic policy in Orissa (1866-1905), 1980, p. 177.
34. T. E. Ravenshaw to Secy., Govt. of Bengal, No. 276, 20 July, 1874, General administration report of Orissa division, 1873-74.
35. Report on the administration of Customs, Department of the Bengal presidency, 1874-75, Sec-V, Para-97, Bengal revenue proceedings, No. 1875.
36. Ibid.
37. Bengal administration report, 1874-75, p. 150.
38. Annual administration report of Bengal presidency for the year 1874-75, Calcutta, 1874, p. 150-151.
39. L.S.S. O' Malley, Bengal district gazetteers (Balasore), Calcutta, 1908, p. 422.
40. Ibid.
41. S. L. Maddox, Final report on the survey and settlement of the province of Orissa, 1890-1900,

Vol. I, p. 7.

42. Report on the administration of Bengal, 1908, Calcutta, 1909, p. 332.

43. L.S.S. O' Malley, op. cit, p. 145.

44. Report on the administration of Bengal 1908-1909, p. 332.

45. Report on the administration of the Customs, Deptt. of the Bengal presidency for 1874-75, Para-101, Bengal revenue proceedings, Nov. 1875.

46. Ibid, Para - 101.

47. A. Smith, Commissioner to Secy., Govt. of Bengal, No. 1369, 5 July, 1879, General administration report of the Orissa division for 1878-79.

48. The figures have been compiled from the various administration report of Orissa division, 1886-1890.

49. These figures have been compiled from the various administration report of Orissa division 1886-1900.

50. R. C. Dutt, The economic history of India, Vol. II, 1976, pp. 252-253. Dadabhai Naoroji, Speeches and writings, pp. 238-239 and Digby, Prosperous British India, London 1891, p. 134.

51. Proceedings of the Bihar and Orissa legislative council, 1920, Speech of Gopabandhu Das in the Budget session for 1918-19.

52. Quoted in "Report on the possibility of establishment of salt industry in the coastal areas of Orissa, 1988, p. 34.

53. Maritime activities and trade in Orissa, Orissa

archieves, Bhubaneswar, 1996, p. 46.

54. S. L. Maddox, op. cit, p. 121.

55. Ibid, p. 138.

56. General administration report of Orissa division, 1877-78.

57. L.S.S. O' Malley, op. cit, pp. 144-145.

Chapter - 5

SALT INDUSTRY

Salt, as an article of general consumption was a staple product of Orissa in the past with which the economic prosperity of the province was virtually connected. *The finest salt of all India*[1] was produced along the extensive seaboard of this province. Its extensive saliferous tract about 320 miles long and 10 to 60 miles broad extended from the river Subarnarekha on the north to the Chilka lake on the south with the eastern Ghat Hill Ranges of the west and the Bay of Bengal to the east was an ideal region for a flourishing salt manufacturing industry. The bounty of nature had placed at the disposal of the people of Orissa an inexhaustible treasure of the sea. Flooded twice in a month by spring tides, the salt lands of Orissa with inexhaustible saline property were singularly well fitted for the manufacture of salt. Adjoining the salt lands the fuel lands on the coast provided sufficient quantities of free fire wood for preparing salt in the boiling process. These advantages had helped in the growth of a rich tradition of salt manufacture and a flourishing salt manufacturing industry on the Orissa coast.

Salt produced in Orissa was of two kinds - *"Panga"* and *"Karkatch"*. Panga salt was obtained by boiling concentrated sea-brine. The boiling process was adopted almost along the entire coast line excepting the estuaries of the Chilka lake in the southern extremity of the province. This was due to the climatic conditions of Orissa coast. It was by the boilng process alone that salt manufacture on the Orissa coast could be protected against frequent showers and thunderstorms. Hence, the boiling process producing *'Panga'* salt had assumed prominence on the Orissa coast. This salt was popular with the consumers for its fineness and bright colour. It enjoyed an extensive market in and outside the province.

Karkatch salt was produced by solar evaporation of sea brine in the estuaries of the Chilka lake. Although crude in quality and dull in colour *karkatch* salt had its importance. It was preferred by certain sections of the people in this province on religious grounds. The sun-dried *karkatch* salt was considered pure for entry into the temples and sacrosanct for religious ceremonies. Like panga, the karkatch variety also enjoyed an extensive market in the Garhjats and the outlying areas to the westward of the province.

As a result of this, an extensive trade in Orissa salt had developed in the past contributing to the prosperity of this province.

During the Maratha rule in Orissa, salt was manufactured in plenty in its coastal areas and had great commercial avenue due to its quality, cheapness and plentiful supply. For this reason it found a ready market in the neighbouring countries to the westward of the province.[2] A considerable salt trade was carried on the river

Mahanadi and its branches with the central provinces, Berar and a host of other countries in that direction.[3] It was the usual practice for the merchants to advance money to *"Malangis"* for manufacturing salt and then they purchased such quantities of the commodity as were produced. If it did not cover the amount advanced, the balance of the money was recovered by instalments. The merchants exported salt to Bengal, Sambalpur, Bihar and other places. Orissa used to export more than three lakh mounds of salt annually during the closing years of the Maratha rule.[4] The Maratha government received only some duty from the salt merchants but did not establish monopoly over the manufacture or sale of salt.[5] No serious thought was given to this essential economic commodity to a systematic administration and make it a source of considerable reference for the state.

Godavarish Mishra in his Anthology; *"Atharasaha Satara"* had said, "In the pre-British period, manufacture and trade in salt was almost free and unrestricted. The poorer folk of the province had been enjoying the privilege of free manufacture of their own consumption. The poorest section of the population in the saliferous tract of the province earned their living by manning salt which they bartered to obtain their household necessities. Some of them, earned a living, as petty retail traders in salt. They carried the articles to every door and sold it cheaply to the people. Under such a system as this, while the poorer sections of the population earned a living, the consumers in general were happy as regards their domestic requirement of salt. The coastal zamindars of the province were allowed to exercise virtual control over the salt affairs of the province. They carried on the manufacture and trade in salt as a profitable business with the help and cooperation of the salt manufacturers and salt merchants. Under this arrangement salt was available cheaply and in plenty throughout the province. Manufacture and sale of salt for the domestic use of the poorer was free and unrestricted. In this way, people in general were comfortable and happy so far as the salt affairs of the province were concerned.

During the Anglo-French war in India large quantities of salt were required for manufacturing ammunitions of war. A greater part of this requirement was met by Orissa salt.[6] So large was the profit from the trade in Orissa salt that merchants could well afford to keep its market price at Rs. 2/- per mound.[7] A flourishing salt trade brought to the Maratha government of Orissa an annual revenue, which exceeded the amount of land revenue, derived by them in this province.[8] The salt trade was so extensive that one Sambhu Bharati, a rich merchant of Cuttack who had bunglows in the different parts of the Khurda region found it worth while to pay for the Khurda Raja his annual pesh-cash of Rs. 10,000/- to the Maratha government on condition of being allowed to conduct his commercial transactions in salt free of all duties and restriction.[9]

British salt monopoly

However, the position changed after the establishment of the British empire in India in 1757. The servants of the East India company carried on trade on this articles paying only a nominal duty after their victory at Plassey. In

1765, Lord Clive formed an *"Exclusive Society"* for inland trade in salt, bettlenut, and tobacco which was confined only to the senior servants of the company. The exclusive society for the first time established complete control on the manufacture of salt.[10]

In 1780 Warren Hastings, the Governor General, recognized the system on a new basis. He appointed several civil officers as salt agents of the company and each officer remained in charge of one agency. They advanced money to the manufacturers of salt or "Malangis" and stored salt and sold it to wholesale, dealers at a price fixed by the government. The company got enough profit from the difference between the price which was received from the wholesale dealers and the amount paid to the "Malangis" for the cost of manufacture.[11]

The eagerness of the British to establish their control over the salt trade of Orissa after the introduction of salt monopoly in Bengal clearly proved the extensiveness of the trade in Orissa. In Bengal, the article was sold at a much higher price than Orissa as the Britishers had established complete monopoly on its manufacture and trade. So they wanted in the first instance to check smuggling of salt from Orissa into Bengal. In 1784, long before the British conquest of Orissa, an order was promulgated to the effect that, no merchant except the company itself, would be allowed to import or sale salt in Calcutta. By such an order, the British government in Bengal clearly intended to exclude the merchants of Orissa, from salt trade in Bengal and thus to give pressure on the Maratha government to allow the company to take control of salt trade in Orissa.[12]

Thus the government had an eye on the flourishing salt trade of Orissa and had tried to extend salt monopoly to the province even before its occupation. There were two reasons for an immediate introduction of the salt monopoly in Orissa. Firstly, the commercial interest of the bengal salt monopoly had to be protected by preventing the cheap Orissa salt entering into the Bengal region. Secondly, the prospects of a flourishing business in Orissa salt had to be exploited to make salt a source of considerable revenue to government. The British rulers, however, adopted a cautions approach in this respect. Unlike in Bengal, they resisted from implementing a full-fleged salt monopoly in this province from the very beginning of its inception in 1804.

After the British possession of Orissa in 1803, they began to organise the salt industry of the region by introducing the monopoly system. The regulation IV of May 1804 reserved to the government the exclusive privilege of manufacturing salt as a source of public revenue. This regulation was enacted by the Governor-General in Council for above noted region with its headquarters at Balasore.[13] The salt manufacture improved under the monopoly system from 1804 to 1863. The average quantity manufactured during these years was 29 lakhs of maunds. After meeting the local requirements, the average amount of salt exported every year by sea in the native crafts to the Sulkia warehouses in Calcutta was about 12 lakhs of maunds. Above all, the extension of manufacture provided means of livelihood to more than 40 thousand people.[14] After the introduction of the salt regulation in 1804, an officer was made the salt agent of Orissa and he was responsible to the Board of Trade, Salt and Opium department at Fort Willium. His duties were to perform the management of the manufacture of salt, the management of the sales for local consumption and the surplus to sulkia and also the prevention of smuggling.

The British divided all the salt aurangs into three divisions, Balasore, on the north Cuttack division, extended from the Subarnarekha on the north to the Dhamra on the south along the western shores of the Bay of Bengal for a distance of some 80 miles and comprised eight aurangs. They were Rattai, Sartha, Chanova, Dusmolung, Panchmolung, Ankura, Churamna and Dhamra.

The central division or Cuttack occupied the central portion of Orissa, extending along the coast of apart 70 miles from the Dhamra to the Devi which separated it from the southern division. It comprised seven Aurangs, Mundamolung, Sathbhaya, northern Kanpur, southern Kanpur, Bankud, southern Dholya and Harishpur. The southern division or Puri occupied the southern portion of Orissa, extending along the coast for about 90 miles from Devi on the north to the south-west extremity of the Chilka lake. It comprised seven Aurangs-north Astaranga, Bhusandapur, Haridas, Parikud, south Astaranga, Malud, Gurbai and Southpara.[15]

The British salt monopoly caused extreme hardship to the poor peasants as it raised the price of salt. It goes without saying that, without the salt monopoly, they could have purchased salt at a much cheaper price. Further, the salt makers, or malangis who were hired by the government to manufacture salt were remunerated at a very low rate. They were forced to work for the government, for many of them had no other means of livelihood. Since they did not receive sufficient remuneration, they had no other choice but to look for opportunities for smuggling.[16]

Under such state of affairs, some experienced english officials recommended for the abolition of salt monopoly, In order to encourage the import of liverpool salt, about the same time, the english merchants put pressure on the Government of Bengal to substitute 'monopoly system' for excise system. In 1863 the salt monopoly was abandoned and excise system was introduced.

Introduction of excise system

Under the *excise system* the licences were allowed to manufacture as much salt as they liked. They sold the salt to the merchants directly and paid the duty and cess to the government before the salt was removed from the storage ground.[17] Thus, after 1863, the salt manufacture was left to the private enterprise under a system of excise. Between 1865-66 and 1882-83 on the average, nearly five lakhs of maunds of salt was manufactured and the license increased from one in 1865-66 to 55 in 1882-83. Simultaneously with the progress of manufacture under the excise system, the government allowed the British salt to enter into Orissa as abundantly as possible.[18]

The liverpool and other imported varieties of salt were unquestionably purer and better in every respect. But up to 1860 none but local salt was known in Orissa. The Oriyas regarded the foreign salt as impure and unfit for use in the land of Gods. No salt of this kind was seen and its exposure for sale would hardly have been tolerated by the ignorant villagers. This prejudice against foreign salt had been completely overcome by 1860. The British salt was sold freely in all the places throughout Orissa. From a variety of causes, such as closing of trade in salt between England and southern states of America, very low freights arising from the American war, a great falling off in the shipments of railway materials and other deed freight, the liverpool salt was imported on a vast scale hence-foreward.[19]

The salt, manufactured under the excise system could not be sold cheaper than the British salt of superior type. The salt producers of Orissa suffered badly and were driven out of their work gradually. Thus, the salt industry of Orissa entered into a crisis and began to decline.

Within a few years of the abolition of the salt monopoly, it was found that not only British salt but also Madras salt was sold in large quantities in many places in Balasore, Cuttack and Puri districts. So long as monopoly system existed, the government tried to oust the cheaper salt from Ganjam. When the monopoly system was abolished, there was a breakdown and Madras traders who flooded the markets of north Orissa. The cheapness of the Ganjam salt sold heavily upon the prospect of the salt manufacture in north Orissa. Under the excise systems, several factors accounted for the costliness of the salt of Orissa as compared to the Ganjam salt (Madras Salt).

The rate of duty on Orissa salt was excessive. Since Orissa formed a division of the Bengal presidency, the duty on Orissa salt was at the

Bengal rate. It was the highest in India. In 1860 the duty on north Orissa salt was Rs. 3.4 whereas the duty on Ganjam salt was Rs. 1.5 annas per mound. W. W. Hunter who visited Orissa in 1870, noticed that the rate was 8s. 8d. per cwt., much higher than the Madras rate was 4s 10d. for an equal quantity. He stated, "now there can be no doubt that, Bengal rate pressed more heavily upon the backward and comparatively poor districts of the Orissa delta than any where in Bengal itself. If there is any single spot in India in which the maximum duty bears too heavily on the people, it is in Orissa."[20]

The price of north Orissa salt was higher than that of Ganjam salt. because, the method of production in Madras (Ganjam) was Karkatch, that is by solar evaporation. In Bengal and in Orissa, the method was Panga, that is by boiling, except in Chilka areas where it was Karkatch. The Panga system was undoubtedly more costly. Besides, the labour employed in making salt was cheaper in Ganjam than in north Orissa.[21]

There was another handicap under which the north Orissa manufacturers were working. As late as 1884, there was a rule in north Orissa requiring the manufacturers to pay for the preventive establishment and warehousing. N. W. Bliss, the commissioner of salt revenue, Madras presidency, in his special reports on Orissa salt in 1884, spoke of this rate as very severe. He stated "it may safely be said therefore that the whole of the salt sold in Orissa during the time, this rule and even more severe predecessors have been in force, has cost the consumer at least two annas 3 paise to 3 annas per maund than it would otherwise have done." In otherwards, the people of Orissa have not only paid government the duty on the salt which they consumed but have paid an additional tax amounting on the whole to the full cost of collecting, that duty from which the people of the rest of India have been exempted." Late Pandit Gopabandhu Das, who is regarded as the Gandhiji of Orissa, rightly observed. "This differential treatment of the industry in Orissa and in its immediate neighbourhood in Madras greatly handicapped and discouraged the Orissa manufacture and caused it gradually to decline.[22]

Because of the factors shown above, the price of the Madras salt was cheaper than that of Orissa Salt. Madras made salt which was smuggled into Orissa was sold at Rs. 2 per maund while north Orissa manufactured salt at Puri was sold at Rs. 2.12 annas per maund. The promulgation of Act X of 1874, introduced a great change in the conditions of salt trade. Free trade in salt was consequently established between north Orissa and Ganjam salt or Madras salt into north Orissa on a large scale. In 1877, in the district of Cuttack, out of every 100 maunds consumed, only five maunds were of local production.[23]

The decline of the salt industry in Orissa was mainly due to the unhealthy competition between liverpool and Madras salt. It was hastened by the lack of proper supervision and unsympathetic attitude of the officers. At a time when the salt manufacturers in Orissa were struggling for bare existence against the mounting expenses for the manufacture of salt, overburdened with numerous salt taxes, selling salt at unremunerative prices, fearing for the unsold and overstocked market, the final deathknell sounded in view of the import of cheap liverpool salt. From 1856 to 1896, the history of salt trade was the tale of an open competition between the indigenous and the foreign salt. It remained only a home industry, unattractive and unremunerative to the people, who began to abandon their home for better job opportunities towards the urban localities.[24] By 1880, the salt industry became extinct in Bengal and lingered uncared for only in the distant coast of Orissa. Pandit Gopabandhu Das remarked "it is not improbable that, the Bengal officers did not like the continuance of the industry in an extreme end by no means attractive in the province, and for want of strict supervision, the excise system which was then working, did not prove a success."[25]

Transfer of Salt administration to Madras

With a view to exercising better supervision over the north Orissa salt manufacture and to prevent illicit practices, the salt administration in Orissa was transferred to the salt department of Madras in 1888. The panga system of manufacture was found costly by the madras authorities in the face of keen foreign competition. In their opinion, it was difficult for supervision and dangerous to the revenue. Panga salt of Balasore could not find a market due to high price consequent upon the enhancement of the rent of the salt lands by the land-owning zamindars. So the making of panga salt was abolished in Orissa in 1889. Manufacture of karkatch salt continued some years longer. In 1891, the excise system under which about 70,000 maunds had been produced per annum on the average, was abolished and the monopoly and direct system was revived under the supervision of Madras salt department, government factories, one at Tua in Puri and the other at Sartha in Balasore and subsequently a third at Gurubai in Puri were opened.[26]

It was expected that the salt industry in Orissa would prosper under the Madras system. But the expectation was disappointed. The Madras authorities did not pay necessary attention to this vital matter. "The Orissa factories observed Pandit Gopabandhu Das," lying as they did at the tail end of the jurisdiction of the madras salt department and outside the presidency, did not receive proper supervision and care from the Madras officers, who naturally attended more to factories situated in the presidency under their immediate supervision."[27] In the opinion of the Madras Board of Revenue, the ignorance of Oriya on the part of the departmental officers was one of the practical difficulties on the way of the successful working of the system of direct manufacture in Orissa.[28]

In these circumstances the Madras officers would be glad to get rid of the troublesome excrescence from their jurisdiction. The question of the retransfer of the Orissa salt department of Bengal came to the forefront. As per the decision of the Government of India, the transfer took effect from 10 October, 1897. The salt trade with Bengal brought prosperity of Orissa. The Balasore district alone exported annually about seven and a half lakhs mounds of salt to the sulkia golas in Calcutta.[29] The panga salt of Balasore was specially popular in Bengal local merchants carried it from the sulkia goals to sale in the interior of that province. The salt office at Balasore was bristling with activity. A flourishing salt trade with Bengal had brought affluence at that time to the people of Balasore in particular and to the province in general. This prosperity lasted until foreign salt invaded Bengal in keen competition with the salt of Orissa. The invasion was backed by political influence from Britain and subsequent encouragement from the government of India. Under pressure from the British mercantile class the Government of India provided more and more facilities to the importers of foreign salt. During the last quarter of the 19th century the avalanche of imported salt entirely displaced Orissa salt from the presidency market in Calcutta. What is more, soon after, Orissa salt was displaced from its own local markets inside the province.

The eventual predominance of the imported salt over the indigenous produce in the Bengal market was foreseen and the Board of Revenue anticipated that the avalanche of imported salt would descend upon Orissa proper. In view of this, suitable sites for the reception and distribution of liverpool salt to meet the internal consumption of the province were earmarked on the Orissa coast.[30] On the Balasore coast Dhamra, Matamadpur and Balliapal and Hansua and false-point of the Cuttack coast were considered to be suitable sites receiving liverpool salt, coming through calcutta. As for the district of Puri, liverpool salt was to land on the Puri beach directly from England.[31]

The first consignment of liverpool salt found its way into Orissa in 1882-83 when 24 mounds of this salt reached Balasore from Calcutta. In the succeeding years if flooded the northern Orissa markets rapidly displacing the local produce.

By 1886-87, the quantity of liverpool salt reaching Balasore went upto 1.40,859, mounds.[32] Out of this, over one lakh mounds were sent to Chandabali. It was distributed in the Cuttack and south Balasore districts. Steamers plying between Calcutta and Orissa ports brought this salt into the markets of this province. There was the decreasing sales of locally manufactured salt and the increasing imported salt coming through Calcutta to displace the indigenous produce in the northern parts of Orissa during the period 1883-84 to 1896-97.[33]

The statement shows that by 1889-90 Cuttack district had ceased to produce any salt for the local market. In the year 1893-94, only 21 mounds of locally made salt were put to sale. By 1894-95 northern Orissa as a whole had ceased to produce any salt for the local market. While Orissa salt was fast disappearing from the local market, the quantity of imported salt registered a steady rise reaching 2,99,836 mounds in 1895-96.[34] Thus, by the year 1896-97, the salt trade of Orissa was thoroughly ruined, confronted by a sweeping on rush of imported salt particularly from liverpool. What Ganjam salt had done to the salt trade in the southern part of Orissa, precisely the same fate befell the salt trade in the northern part of the province on account of the liverpool salt.

In short, the salt trade of Orissa in general was squeezed out of existence by the invasion of liverpool salt from the north and Ganjam salt from the south. The destruction of the salt trade produced ruinous effects on the economy of the province and the general welfare of her people.

While this sort of chaos reigning in the administration, the local manufactures were contracted from year to year. When the East Coast railway was opened, the competition by the Ganjam and liverpool salt was intensified and Orissan salt' was unable to hold its own." The Sartha factory was closed in 1893 and Tua and Gurubai factories were closed in the beginning of 1898. Thus salt which was once an established industry in the coastal areas of Balasore, Cuttack and Puri districts finally came to a close.

The statement shows how the sale of locally manufactured salt was diminishing and that of imported salt was increasing between 1887-88 and 1896-97.

Year	Sales of locally manufactured salt			Sales of imported salt			Total
	Balasor	Cuttack	Puri	Ganjam	Calcutta	Madras	
1	2	3	4	5	6	7	8
1887-88	29335	33408	120476	858292	188811	-	729962
1888-89	-	1757	123758	346327	192165	-	664007
1889-90	620	-	80466	413165	238690	-	730941
1890-91	1908	-	128664	311257	284033	-	725862
1891-92	826	-	18440	443071	251971	-	713908
1892-93	13859	-	67470	337423	276408	-	695160
1893-94	21	-	24439	446040	285934	2883	759817
1894-95	-	-	33715	351714	275764	-	666193
1895-96	-	-	74635	994326	299836	-	668797
1896-97	-	-	46224	395196	280885	-	722205

(Source : Report on the possibility of establishment of salt industry in the coastal areas of Orissa, 1938, p. 12)

The result of the destruction of the salt industry proved harmful to Orissa. It threw a trading community of coastal Orissa out of employment. Dislocation of any single community from its proper economic position affected other economic groups. Consequent upon the extinction of salt industry, nearly 40 thousand people in Balasore, Cuttack and Puri districts were deprived of their means of livelihood. Pandit Gopabandhu Das rightly observed "When I see the great body of labourer suffering year by year for want of employment and hopelessly leaving their wives and children, going out to Burma and Assam in quest of wages, I cannot but bewall the loss, Orissa has sustained at the hands of officers who should have looked at the situation with sympathy, a liberal spirit and in a statesman like way."[35]

Revival of salt industry in Orissa

During the closing years of the 19th century and early years of the 20th century, the condition of the great majority of the inhabitants of coastal Orissa had gone from bad to worse. The perpetual scarcity forced many of them to leave for Bengal in search of employment. So the necessity for the revival of Salt industry arose to provide labour to thousands of poverty-stricken Oriyas. It was estimated that 4,000 acres atleast could be available in Orissa coast for salt factories and when they were fully developed not less than half a lakh of people would find employment, Carett, then collector of Puri stated "The revival of salt manufacture, it could be brought about, would be of advantages to the people of this district, and I am in favour of it. It would be of special benefit to the inhabitants of the Chilka tracts where the crops were frequently liable to failures. Salt manufacture would also be a source of employment for the people during the hot weather months where the work of any kind is very difficult to procure."[36]

In 1901 and in 1908, the question of reviving the manufacture of salt was considered by the board of revenue and government. In the enquiry of 1901, the change of revival of salt manufacture in the Chilka area was not declared. Sri K.G. Gupta, Commissioner of Excise, Bengal, noted "The revival of manufacture is thus feasible only in the small area comprised in the Chilka where conditions though not very favourable, are not altogether inimical to Karkatch manufacture."

During the first World War, the question acquired a new importance. The high price of salt then prevailing rendered the prospects of reviving the industry much more favourable. F.W. Gooch investigated into the commercial aspects of such revival. He thought that, the revival of manufacture by karkatch method on the Chilika lake might be successful but he was not so hopeful of panga method due to changed circumstances."[37]

The representatives of the people had brought forward the question of revival in Orissa on several occasions in the provincial and central legislatures. The most able and convincing speech of Pandit Gopabandhu Das in Bihar and Orissa legislative council made on 13 March 1918, could make the government admit that the stoppage of salt manufacture caused immense hardship to the agricultural population of coastal Orissa. The government assured that, due attention would be paid to the question of the revival of the salt industry in Orissa.[38]

In this speech, Gopabandhu Das elaborately discussed how it was quite possible for starting an industry in the Chilka area for the following reasons. Firstly, the salt producing capacity of the Chilka area was a historic fact. The annual yield of this area alone amounted at one time to over six lakhs of maunds and rose in some years to nearly 10 lakhs of maunds. Secondly, the initial cost for opening the manufacture would not be much, for the salt pans and crystallizing beds lie there too well-marked and might be made ready for work with a comparatively small outlay. Thirdly, the labourers would never be wanting and might be had on cheaper wages. Men of the Chilka tract were then working in the neighbouring factory at Huma (then in Madras). They would gladly come back to fields close to their homes for less wages. There were many without employment, who knew the process of manufacture. Fourthly, the output of salt in the Chilka area would not be less than that of neighbouring areas in Ganjam (in Madras). At Huma the area under operation was 900 acres and at Surla nearly 450. The annual yield per acre at Humma was about 800 maunds and that at Surla nearly 700 mounds. There was no reason why the Chilka factories if properly managed could not produce almost the same amount. Lastly, in the salt manufacturing season, that is during the period from December to the end of May, the brine of Eram at Balasore, Astarang in Puri and Tua and Gurubai of Chilka area was sufficiently strong.[39]

Gopabandhu Das, one of the makers of modern Orissa, gave a concrete suggestion on how the salt manufacture in the Chilka area was to be revived. An experimental factory might be started over an area of 300 acres. It should be worked on the government nonopoly system. When found successful, it would certainly appeal to some enterprising people who would come forward to manufacture salt under the excise system. The private capitalists should however be encouraged from the beginning to undertake the work side by side with the government factory. Afterwards, the government factory might be leased out to private person on such terms as might be then considered fair and necessary. Late Gopabandhu Das expressed emphatically "if factories are started on this line not only in the Chilka but through out the Orissa coast, Madras salt can never make its way into the province. All that wanted is a steady consistent policy to be purchased in the belief that the industry which once proved successful may again be worked with advantage for the people and the state."[40]

Agitation continued for the revival of the industry but without any success.

Effects of the destruction of salt trade

Salt trade was an important item absorbing labour and capital of the region and it had profound impact on the major portion of the population of Orissa. Out of the revenue derived from taxation by the British government the salt duty constituted the biggest single item as it was much higher than the land revenue of the province. But the destruction of salt industry, because of the heavy taxation and importation of Ganjam and liverpool salt led to the economic ruination of Orissa in general. This ruination affected the people of Orissa specially (1) Disappearance of the coastal shipping and the ship building industry. It led thousands of sailors, khalasis, carpenters, smiths, cartner and host of others unemployed, (2) Ruination of all the subsidiary trades which thrived on the salt trade like the merchandise of rice and transportation, (3) Abandonment and desertion of the port of Balasore.

During the hey-day of the salt trade, coastal shipping was in a prosperous state in northern Orissa. Nearly three hundred ships were engaged in this trade. On an average of fifteen persons per ship, more than four thousand persons were employed as sailors, khalasis, etc. in the craft of this province. In addition to this, there were carpenters, smiths, cartmen and a host of others who found employment in ship building industry.[41] All the merchants and owners of ships belonged to Balasore. Their prosperity was dependent on this industry. The cessation of the salt trade ruined this industry and its dependents, all kinds of sea-going vessels plying between Orissa ports and other places. They were never rebuilt nor new ones made.[42] The sailors as a class, a part of whom were already effaced from the face of the earth during the Orissa famine of 1866 were now thoroughly ruined. The commissioner of Orissa Mr. T.E. Ravenshaw describing the condition of the province in 1867 wrote, "The disruption of trade and communication between the ports of Orissa and Calcutta resulted in the rotting of sloops in the creeks; even river boats and boatmen disappeared. In the absence of adequate number of boats immense difficulties were faced by the government in importing rice for the famine stricken people of Orissa"[43]

Although the coast craft of Orissa was mainly engaged in the salt trade of the province, it had also promoted a few other subsidiary trades at the same time. Its sea going vessels transacted business in several other merchandise not only with the port of Calcutta but with several other southern ports such as Gopalpur, Vizagapatam and Madras. The subsidiary trades disappeared immediately following the destruction of the salt trade. The people of Balasore and Orissa in general possessing very little capital for fresh investment were reduced in poverty. Their business passed into the hands of outsiders coming from the neighbouring provinces.[44] Thereafter, the people of Orissa could never retrieve their former prosperity.

The once famous port of Balasore which had prospered mainly due to the salt trade lost its importance. The prosperity which the district in general and the business community in particular enjoyed on account of the salt trade was then reflected in the flourishing port of Balasore. Since long Balasore had attained a prominent place among the ports in the eastern sea board of India.[45] The early europeans had established their factories here much before Calcutta had become the seat of their trade and commerce.[46] The Budhabalanga river near Balasore was seen dotted with ships from different parts of the world.[47] But the destruction of the salt trade struck at the very root of the prosperity of Balasore. Consequently, the port ceased to be a rendezevous of ships, sailor and businessmen. It presented a deserted and desolate look and hence, appeared to be a grave-yard of the once flourishing salt trade of this province.

To sum up, the disappearance of the salt trade led to a serious economic setback throughout the province. The poor masses of this flood stricken state lost their prime source of maintenance. The condition of the middle classes also deteriorated on this score. Even Zamindars with their share in the salt trade had prospered during the hey-day of this trade, were eliminated from the field of commerce, following the destruction of the salt trade. In general, decay, despair and misery stalked the land. Attempts were made by the provincial government to revive it but the revival proved to be a cry in the wilderness due to the unwillingness of the central government. Consequently, resentment was general all over the province and consequently this discontent was manifested in the shape of an agitation against the salt policy of the government culminating in the salt satyagraha of 1930.

COTTAGE INDUSTRY

Although agriculture formed the main feature of the economic life of the people, yet, there existed several crafts and industries in Orissa during the period under survey. Traditional craft of Orissa represents its glorious heritage of creative art which was intermingled with her religion, philosophy and way of life. Artisans involved in production of things of utility had revealed their artistic ingenuity and sensibility every thing they produced. As it seems, a considerable portion of Orissa's population earned their livelihood working as manufactures of various kinds of agriculture and non-agricultural products. The abundance of products was such that even after the full needs of the people were met, there was left considerable surplus for export.

Due to non-introduction of modern industrial system of production, India in general and Orissa in particular continued to witness practically a primitive and stagnant mode of production. However, cottage industries were of great importance for the economic development of the masses who were employed for only half the time in agriculture. The artisans were generally confined to villages and were engaged in supplying the needs of the agricultural population. They were not acquainted with the modern process of efficient production and the application of labour-saving devices. They did not know how best to utilise the raw materials and how to cheapen production. The use of improved appliances were unknown to most of the artisans. In course of time the influx of foreign goods led to the decay of the cottage industries. But they did not meet with total extinction as the Oriyas had strong likings for locally manufactured things.

The epic refers to eighteen craft associations such as jewellers, potters, ivory carvers, performers, goldsmith, weavers, brass-makers, painters, musical instrument makers, armorers, leather workers, blacksmiths, carpenters, coppersmiths, makers of figures, cutters, glass makers and in layers.[48] Orissa continued to be a store house of handicraft goods, handicrafts including textile constituted a mojor item of import from India. Besides textiles, filigree works, brass and metal work, bamboo work, cane work, pottery, tanning, cart making, tolly-making, calico painting, carpentry, etc. were other important handicrafts of Orissa.[49]

Cotton weaving

Cotton weaving was the most important cottage industry of Orissa. The cotton products of Orissa received high appreciation in Europe.[50] The village weavers used to manufacture their products through tantas (handmade looms). The weavers were identified in the society as tantis. Cotton weaving was carried out in three districts of Cuttack, Puri and Balasore by tantis.They continued to weave coarse cotton cloth which cost was much higher than the imported cloth from England.[51] The important places of weaving in Orissa were Gulnagar in Kendrapada sub-division in Cuttack district, Dhala pathar in Khurda sub-division of Puri district, Ragadi in Banki sub-division in the district of Cuttack and Bhadrak in Balasore district.[52]

Handloom weaving was the most important cottage industry in Orissa and it was spread all over the region. Some of the cotton-weavers exhibited considerable taste in colour and variety of pattern and the textile goods made by such workers were highly appreciated. Some of the screens and table cloths produced were so very artistic in design that there was a demand for them from outside markets including even foreign countries like Sweden. Sometimes, the products of this weaving industry were not merely sold in the localities but were also sent to markets for sale.[53]

The weaving industry of Orissa was in a state of decline during the British reign. The condition of weaving industry in Orissa has been described by P.T. Mansfield as follows, "Weaving is not carried as an organised industry but in the homes of the weavers themselves who are also frequently agriculturists when the yarn is purchased the women and children do the wandering of the warps and this is no mean contribution for the warping of sufficient ends which involves a walk of ten miles. There is no regular system and no fixed hours of work, the weavers often work early and late but seldom in the lot of the day.[54]

The weaving industry in Orissa did not thrive in the face of competition with cheaper imported fabrics. There was some demand for "Tassar cloth for its texture and durability. European machine made cloths which were superior in texture, durability and were comparatively cheaper in value captured the market. These were imported by weekly steamers from Calcutta to Chandabali and to the false-point and distributed from Cuttack. Bombay machine made piece goods chiefly dhoties were preferred by poor people owing to its durability. Most of the weavers of

Cuttack district who were once famous for their manufacture gave up their profession and were ruined. Out of 37,822 weavers according to the census of 1872 A.D, only four were assessed in 1880-81 under the License Act. In 1901-02, there was no manufacturing importance in Orissa.[55] The industry was languishing at the end of the Maratha rule, the decline was complete with the coming of British rule with its colonial interest.[56]

This industry was a source of employment to a large number of weavers. As Orissan soil was not suitable for cotton cultivation, bales of cotton wool were imported to Orissa from Berar and black soil cotton belt of Maharastra through the land route of Raipur-Sambalpur. The accounts of T. Motte gives a graphic description to it. The cotton bales were exported to Orissa in lieu of her cheap rice and salt.[57] The Maratha government gained from cotton trade by imposing heavy customs duty making it costly. The cotton cultivation discouraged with a view to surplus rice of Orissa to Nagpur.[58]

Towards the last quarter of the 18th century, the British residents at Cuttack found the flourishing textile industry in the province and decided to invest money in it and settled some Bengali weavers around Balasore, Jajpur and Bhadrak. G.P. Leckie in March 1790 passing through Balasore on his way to Nagpur found that Orissa textile industry was waning.[59] After the British conquest, there was a bid to increase the volume of revenue receipt which compelled the government to impose heavy customs duty on trade commodities. The imposition of heavy custom duty on cotton bales of Nagpur and importation of english cotton yarns brought decline of cotton trade between Nagpur and Orissa. The decline of cotton textile industry had a direct effect on cotton cultivation in 19th century. The following table reveals the decline of cotton cultivation in Cuttack district between 1833-1897.

Table 1 : Decline of cotton cultivation in Cuttack district (1883-1897)

Year	Area in acres
1833	3020
1858	6474
1877	7935
1894-95	6100
1895-96	5900
1896-97	5300

Madhusudan Das and Swami Bichitrananda Das introduced Charkha (Spinning wheel) in 1903 which was piled formerly in every household in Orissa. They encouraged the cotton cultivation to save the people from hard competition with west and to save the weavers as well as cultivators from hard competition with Manchester goods.[60] After 1905, government took interest in reviving the handloom industry by training the weavers in up-to-date methods of weaving and supplying the modern implements required for the purpose and reasonable prices.[61] Therefore, industrial schools established in Balasore district. The Alarpur Industrial School of Balasore was established in 1889.[62] Weaving, carpentry and blacksmith training were taught to the pupils. Balasore technical school was managed by American Baptist Mission. All the trainees found employment in various industries. It proved to be futile due to want of yarn. Though only 5000 mounds of cotton was produced from 8000 acres of land, the fate of the weaver population received a little change.[63]

Tassar weaving

The tassar silk industry was one of the indigenous industry of Orissa. This small scale industry was carried on in the villages of Gopalpur, Dharmasala, in the Cuttack district. There were 600 persons engaged in this industry.[64] Tassar cloth was manufactured in some parts of Puri district. It received a serious set back by interference of the forest department which tried to stop tassar rearing in the forest of Orissa. Tassar rearing was common in the forests of Angul, Sukinda and other estates. They were more costly more for their durability than for their fairness. This weaving industry can hardly thrive in the face of cheaper machine made Manchester fabrics.[65]

Brass and Bell-Metal

The brass and bell-metal craft was the traditional and major. Orissan cottage industry which provided employment to about 2,000 artisan families scattered in various parts of the state. The articles of metalcraft consists of household utensils, large vessels and decorative pieces. Utensils were made out of an alloy of copper and zinc. Bell-metal was the composition of tin, bronze containing upto 30 percent tin and some zinc and lead. This mixture of metals called Kansa was of extensive use in manufacturing utensils. Bell-metal and brass ornaments were also of extensive use amongst the women in Orissa.[66] The brass and bell-metal workers were called kansari or thatari. Ghantimunda in Cuttack district, Balakati in Puri district and Remuna in Balasore were famous for making kansa and brass utensils.[67] Kantilo in Puri district was also manufacturing utensils of brass and bell-metals.[68] Bhuban in Dhenkanal district was also famous for this industry. Ghantimunda in Cuttack district does embroidery work on brass metal.

The products of the bell-metal were broadly classified into three groups items produced through the process of beating known as (pita), those produced by casting and third group includes the rest items. The workshop of the bell metal workers was called 'sala' consisting of a platform with a block of stone on which neating was done, a heating furnace (bhati) to polish it. The tools used in the crafts were hammers and anvils, pinurs, hand drills, files and scraffers. The items manufactured thrast the beding process were plates (thali), flat around container (Kansa), small container (Gina), tumblers, water container (Gara), buckets, large cooking utensils, storage vessels (hands) and various types of pots and pans. The plates used as house hold utensils and for puja were engraved with flora and geometric designs, human and animal figures, increasing the decorative values of the objects.

Brass casting was done by the Kansaris and the items produced were icons of Radha, Krishna, Durga, Lakshmi, Ganesh, Vishnu, Bells, lamp stands, lamp, etc. Bronze casting and old craft was no longer in practice in Orissa although the craft reached the highest water mark in the past as was evident from discovery of a large number of bronze icons from Banapur of Puri and from Ratnagiri of Cuttack district. During the 'Ratha Yatra' or car festival, hundreds of the songs were beaten rhythmically by the devotees and priests in frenzied ecstasy as the divine chariots were pulled forward by the thronging millions.[69] Since the coming of cheap aluminium articles, this indigenous industry was seriously affected. This industry could not die altogether as it had a special use in the temples and was a great demand on a list of dowry articles at the time of the marriage. The musical instruments, Jhanja and Kubuji were manufactured. Brass and bell-metal utensils, ornament wires were exported to Calcutta from Chandabali port. This industry has a long continuing tradition from the ancient times.

Filigree

Filigree was one of the finest specimens in jewellery, usually made in every thin silver, sometimes in gold which has a soft foamy appearance and a dainty spider-web delicacy. Silver filigree was made in three leading centres of India, Cuttack in Orissa, Karimnagar in Andhra Pradesh and Murshidabad in West Bengal.[70] Silver filigree was called the queen of Orissan finer crafts.

This craft is localised at Cuttack town and a few villages in the district. In view of the long continuing craft, the artisans had developed high sense of ingenuity, dexerity and workmanship and at present, the craft is almost in a boon having markets in India and abroad. This industry afforded employment to about 400 families in Cuttack town and more than 2000 families of rural areas in the districts.[71]

The craft was locally known as tarakasi. The raw materials used in the craft were pure silver-diamond and gold dust were available from the river ibid and Mahanadi. Gold was found from the bed of the Trika river near Angul and in the river Brahmani and the Subarnarekha beds.[72] Goldsmith of Orissa made use of this gold in making ornaments as required by the customers. The workers used to prepare fine delicate knotted specimens of gold and silver ornaments. The first variety of ornaments for ladies which may be necklaces, broches anklets, hair-pins, decorative key rings, hangers, etc. The decorative items were boats, chariots, replicas of temples, horses, elephants, lions and other animals. The last variety comprising useful items were plates, cups, bowls, glasses, containers, indigenous spoons, vermilion container, etc. The bowls, glasses and other utensils made of silver was used in feeding the solid food to the child on the occasion of *Anna Prasana.*[73] Silver filigree had been one of the most important item of export to foreign countries.

To develop the filigree industry Late. M.S. Das the pioneer of modern industry established the *"Orissa Artwares"* by utilising the inherent skill of the workers for production of articles accounting to the present taste of the people. Specimens of filigree work were sent to Paris exhibition. In 1900, he advertised *"Orissa Artwares"* which he established with a view to expanding the cottage and traditional small scale industries in Orissa.[74] In order to organise the industry on scientific basis and to improve the crafts government sponsored organisation known as Kalinga filigree works which has been set up at Cuttack. It has now become the main centre of research production and marketing within the country and abroad and has been able to provide jobs to a large number of workers. The craft, confined previously to the goldsmith caste, is now patronised by those who are interested in the line. The training programme of craftsmen by the crafts institute Bhubaneswar run by the industry department further accelerate the cause of filigree crafts.[75]

Horns

The art of making articles in animal horns was as old as the civilisation itself. The horns of buffalo, cattle, deer, sambar and bison constituted the raw material of the craft. The adivasis and the scheduled castes people living in jungle and hilly areas supplied the raw materials to the craftsmen who belonged to the carpenter caste having the surname of Maharana.[76] Horn works have great utilisation and decorative values. The traditional items were combs of various types such as oil, comb, snuff-box, hair-pin, walking stick with animal designs on the handles, wall-flower vase, clips, tongue cleaner, wall hanger, shoe-horn, knife with decorative designs and tobacco pipes. The new items of object were animal figure like crane, prawn, crap, lizard fish, scorpion butterfly, birds, etc. table lamp, stand, pen stand, cigarette holder, statue of gods and goddesses, etc. Horn and ivory articles of Orissa were exported to Calcutta, Bombay and many other places. The horn traders earned their livelihood regularly by making horn articles.[77]

Applique works

The applique work was in a flourishing state linked with a high degree of technical skill and imagination. This craft was mainly concentrated at Pipli, a village on the Jagannath trunk road, thirty kilometers from Bhubaneswar and forty kilometers from Puri. The applique craft had a long history and was closely connected with the rituals and traditions of Lord Jagannath. The applique workers were the sevakas of the Jagannath temple as they had supplied applique to the temple. The applique items like Chhatitarass and Chandua were mainly used during the procession of deities.[78]

Stone carving

E.B. Havell in the monography "Stone Carving in Bengal" published in 1906, said that within the area in Bengal as a stone building country, Orissa was excellent.[79] Carvers were acquired the most extraordinary technical skill erecting temples by stone in the district of Cuttack and Puri. The Director General of Archeological Survey in 1902-03 said that the work of the modern stone, mason, a native of Bhubaneswar and of surrounding places did not lag behind the old working style.[80] The stone carvers of Orissa one day had excelled others in producing bold effects of light and shade that made a statue more lively. Thus, the stone carvers, the wage earner group were superior to the stone artisans of european countries and number of stone carvers were getting their subsistence out of this cottage industry.

Jute

Jute spun into strings was vitally needed for many useful articles. At Bant, Basudevpur and many other places in the district of Balasore, people made excellent gunny bags for the use of packs. These handmade gunny bags were much more durable than the millmade products.

Beautifully coloured door mats, durries and staircase runners were manufactured these days with jute strings. These articles were cheaper than those made with costly yarns. The small durries could serve the purpose of a bed or a mat for the poor villager. The cottage industries taught people how to weave the durries. The process was so simple that any villager could weave it in his own home.[81]

Rope making

The village homes and cultivators used a considerable quantity of rope for drawing water, and for agricultural purpose. But they mostly made their own ropes or got it locally made by some of the low caste men in the villages who made coir ropes. The chief materials used for rope making in north Orissa were jute, indian and sisal hemps, coir and some grasses. The quantity of sisal hemp available was small but jute and coir were available in plenty. But for want of suitable organisation and effort to encourage rope-making on a large scale as a cottage industry, Orissa had to import a considerable quantity of ropes and strings. Many expressed the view that it would be profitable to encourage rope-making as a spare time occupation for the cultivators who had not get enough to keep them occupied throughout the year.

Oil milling

Oil was manufactured, both for lighting and cooking purposes, from mohwa, caster, til, genially and niger seeds. The process was either by grinding in the usual wooden mill or by simply squeezing the seeds between two boards. The needs of the rural population were served by a class of people known as "Teli" whose family occupation was to press and deal in "Tel", i.e,. oil They were found all over the state as they were the people who supplied the oil used in cooking food. The village "Teli" used bullock-driven wooden oil presses. They were now meeting with a serious competition from oil mills, and the age old profession was gradually dying out.[82]

Potteries

Pottery manufacture was one of the most important village industries in Orissa. The potter's clay was widely distributed in Orissa and was used for the manufacture of cook in pots water vessels, and pots of various shapes and sizes for storing foodgrains and for numerous other uses. The articles made by the village potters were universally used in all homes in Orissa both by the rich and the poor. At so many places the village potters made also roofing, flooring and ceiling tiles, drain pipes and earthenware rings for wells.

Some of the village potters worked also as brick-layers and toy-makers. The toys, made specially at Cuttack, were quite artistic in design and could find a market outside.[83]

Wood work and furniture

The manufacture of wooden articles such as furniture, boxes, packing cases, doors, windows, shelves & tool handles, etc. was carried on by a large number of people all over Orissa. In the district of Cuttack alone, there were about 3,000 carpenters. Carpentry played a very important role in village life and organisation as it supplied all tools, and appliances needed for village crafts. The village carpenters also did the work of building and repairing houses and agricultural implements. They were generally paid in kind for doing these hereditary works. Furniture making was mostly confined to towns and its chief centre in Orissa was Cuttack where some 300 families were engaged in this occupation. Here the profession had been taken up by the people of other hereditary carpenters. The carpenters of Cuttack town had more than a local reputation for their skill in furniture making. In Ganjam district very skilled carpenters were found. They supplied furniture to Calcutta and other places where their workmanship was appreciated.[84]

Toys

Toy-making was an important art in Orissa Cuttack town was famous for its toys. Clay toys from Cuttack were sold in all parts of Orissa and the neighbouring provinces. The manufacture of unbreakable toys was an innovation of the poor cottage industries at Cuttack. The articles were sold not only in Orissa but also there was a demand for them from the central provinces, like Berar, Bombay and Delhi. The industry ought to be put on a commercial basis so as to meet the growing demands.[85]

Cane Work

Cane grew throughout the district of Cuttack and Puri in abundant measure. Cane was used in the rural areas in Orissa for tying the bamboo frame work of thatched roofs and for making baskets and furniture to meet the needs of villagers. Dampara in the Cuttack district and Banapur in the Puri district were two chief centres of production of cane articles, as the best varieties of cane were grown in these localities. The cane seats and backs of chairs etc. were woven by some of the workers who lived in or around these areas. Cuttack jail and the Madhusudan village industries institute made varieties of cane articles, such as chairs, tables, baskets and trays, etc. There was a demand for these articles as they were light and handy but there sufficient number of trained workers were not available to make the articles according to modern designs and taste.[86]

Mat weaving

Mats were needed in every home in Orissa and there was great scope for organising mat weaving as a cottage industry. Mats were made out of reeds, of grass, jute and coir, all of which were available in plenty in Orissa. The particular types of mate known as "Sapa" were greatly in demand. Sapas were made in some villages in north Balasore mostly confined to the Bhograi police-station, where the aquatic plants were used in making mats grew in abundance. It was said that mats worth several thousand rupees were exported from this area by rail, road and river to other parts of Orissa and Bengal. Mats made with seasoned white reeds were more lasting and fetched better price than those made with fresh reeds. But most of the mat weavers, were poor landless labourers and petty cultivators. They could not stock sticks for seasoning them.[87]

Smelting of Iron and steel as a cottage industry

The "loharies" of village blacksmiths had smelted local deposits of iron ore throughout Orissa for centuries. Although imported iron was available, smelting of iron was done at some localities chiefly in the inaccessible areas in the hilly tracts of Ganjam and Koraput. The "loharies" used mostly soft and inferiors grades of iron ore which could not be used for iron smelting in the big iron works in India.

The Ganjam iron ore was reported in certain localities such as the Kaladhar Parbat ne. Kodala and at Bari and Barada in Ghumsur sub-division and in the Khondmala. In Koraput people belonging to the two castes called "Khati" and "Lohar" manufactured some iron by their crude process, and made with it the tools and implements required by the simple village folk.

Hide industry

Another important article of export from Orissa was hide. The dense forests of Orissa afforded plenty of opportunity for this trade. The spread of leather industry in northern India demanded plenty of hides from different parts of India. The business community rushed to Orissa to take advantage of the availability of hides in large quantity. Cuttack district done exported 13,979 pieces of hides at a cost of Rs. 23,053 during the year 1869-70.[88] During the year 1876-77 Balasore port exported 1,39,863 pieces Cuttack exported 74,234 pieces and Puri exported 2,14,106 pieces of hides to different places.[89] The communities which collected animal skins preferably big animals belonged to the lowest caste of the society. Shoe-makers known as 'mochis' were found generally in small and big towns. These families were getting their bread from the hide industry in Orissa.

The business of northern India exploited the situation and engaged their agents for the collection of hides from interior junglee villages of Orissa. The 'mochis' who were manufacturers of leather goods could not withstand the competition when the north India business mean were ready to give high prices for the hides. Many leather workers were thrown into unemployment though the middlemen belonging to Orissa engaged for the procurement of hides were benefited. Consequent upon the export of hides in large quantity from Orissa, the leather cottage industry declined which was again reflected on the economy of this group of families. This change in the trend of hide business crippled the local leather industry.[90] The Utkal Tannery, the first organised leather industry also received the same injury for its decline.

Stone quarry industry

There were no mines of importance in Orissa. Laterite, sand stones and lime stones were quarried from the hills and were used for road metalling and building purposes. Following the years of famine, the government changed the economic policy and resolved to allot more funds for the construction of good all-weather roads. Completion of Bengal-Nagpur railway lines was decided by the government. Construction work was expedited by stones mainly from Chaudwar quarries and from quarry around Dharmasala for the construction of railway bridges.[91] The owners of these mines had done handsome business with the authorities of the Bengal-Nagpur railway company. The following statistics gives a clear picture about the amount of business transaction of different years in store.[92]

Year	Amount
1896	Rs. 15,703.00
1897	Rs. 94,852.00
1898	Rs. 6,10,149.00
1899	Rs. 3,35,231.00

Out of these figures it can be firmly said that stone quarry industries continued to provide employment to a large number of workers in Orissa.

Causes of decline of the cottage industries

Orissa was once a great manufacturing nation whose industrial products had supplied for centuries the needs of vast asian and european markets. The spinning and weaving and other handicrafts had provide whole-time or part-time employment to millions of men and women. But all this gradually disappeared with the advent of the British rule and Orissa had lost not only its foreign markets but also its internal markets and had started importing foreign manufactures in a large scale. The East India company also used its political power to acquire monopolistic control over weavers and other handicrafts men and to force them to produce goods at cheap and uneconomic, prices, thus, compelling them to abandon their ancestral profession.[93]

Multifarious factors were responsible for decay of handicrafts and cottage industries during the British rule of Orissa.

Influx of foreign goods, the construction of railways by the end of the 19th century, lack of organisation,. financial constraints, competition with large scale industries and foreign goods all combinedly signalled the decay of cottage industries of Orissa. Thousands of rural artisans lost their traditional livelihood and became agricultural labourers. This indicated the deep poverty of the people which compelled to migrate in search of livelihood. The Oriyas had already deserted their houses. Children and wives were wandering in quest of employment in other provinces.[94]

The weavers, the potters, the chamaras, the mochis, the carpenters, the goldsmiths, the damas and other professional hereditary skilled-workers were always busy in manufacturing their articles to meet the local demands. The did never think to produce qualitative goods to face competition with machine-made finished goods. Weaving, hide and paper industries were facing a lot of competition with the finished goods of cheap rates imported by the english administration. Thus, Britishers apathy coupled with import of cheap foreign goods led to the decline of cottage industries in Orissa.

Another important factor for the decline of industries in Orissa was the absence of good markets for the sale of articles. The products were sent by the manufacturers to nearby hats for sale twice a week. Robert Ker was the first British officer who felt the necessity of an open market. His initiative resulted with the opening of a public market in Cuttack town.[95] The manufacturers were to depend on the local hats to sell the articles where there was no competitive and where the articles were purchased by the traders or intermediaries at a lower price and sent them to urban markets to sell at higher price thus squeezing the economic gain of the manufacturers.[96] The absence of free and open markets inside and outside Orissa led the decline of the indigenous village industries.

The British administration turned a deaf year to the improvement of communication facilities for Orissa. Orissa was virtually an isolated tract till 1897 when East Coast railway line was ready for traffic.[97] When easy and a cheaper communication facilities were not available the manufacturers neither were able to procure raw materials from distance places at cheap rate nor could sell the articles in urban markets at higher rate. Under these conditions the artisans of Orissa were forced to remain at the mercy of local traders and were forced to accept a low price below the production cost.

The prosperity of industry and the growth of trade was directly connected to the currency system. Kauris were the medium of exchange during the Maratha rule and in earlier times.[98] During the first phase of the British rule, the scarcity of Kauris was felt as the army people were paid heavy through Kauris. And also the pilgrims visiting Orissa were pressing had for kauri currency.[99] This was evident from the letter of harcourt to Mr. Shaw, private secretary to the Governor-General ;"We are very much distressed for want of small coins or Kauris."[100] The question of currency system did not receive proper attention of the government and there were troubles in business transactions. There was the depreciation of Kauries per rupees like 7 kahans per one rupee. The village artisans were not willing to sell their products on rupee. As a result, the products of village industries of Orissa could not be displayed in the markets of any other provinces. The period of stagnancy came in and local industries started declining.

The great famine desperately dislocated the economic condition of the people of Orissa. The artisans tried their utmost to revive their industries but the appearances of famines at short intervals ruined them. As a result, they became unable to pay back the loans. After the famine the price index gradually went up. The rise in price of foodgrains had tremendous impact on the industries. The artisans used to earn less and were required to pay more for foodgrains and other articles. During the period from 1814 to 1890, there was 50% rise in money wages for an ordinary worker and there was 125 percent rise in price of the cost of living.[101] The purchasing capacity of an individual diminished to a great extent. This was reflected on the village based industries. The artisans became the worst sufferers due to abnormal price rise of foodgrains which led its decline.

The influx of rich Bengalis to Orissa as land-lords adversely affected the growth of industries in Orissa. The Bengalis had money but they had no interest to invest capital on industry rather they were busy in diverting their capital to Bengal market. They drained their raw materials to Calcutta and earned their fortune. On the other hand, the government did not care for this nor was interested to patronise the local industries. When the administration was callous and failed to formulate any industrial policy and major capital investment and the self-centered landlords of Bengal having no interest to patronise local industries and the manufacturers being penniless following the onslaught of famines, it could be sheer foolishness to set up better industries in Orissa.

Above all, the British administration was responsible for the decline of cottage industries in Orissa. British administration did not pay any attention to the development of communications in Orissa. Most of the regions of Orissa remained inaccessible forests. Britishers were ignorant about the economic system of the people and the country. This is one of the vital reasons why many of the economic problems, concerning industry, trade and commerce could not be examined by competent authorities. Therefore, Orissa had to suffer from the maladjustment of the industrial economy whereas the other provinces marched ahead on the path of economic prosperity and industrial growth.

The monopolistic theory of the British administration worked very effectively in Orissa in relation to industry. The company as a trading community became busy in exporting raw materials to England and importing english finished goods to Orissa. The weaving industry and salt industry faced a stiff competition with machine-made english goods in the markets. Metal industry was compelled to be closed as all the raw materials were drained for their use. The manufactures could not withstand the competitive markets. As a result of which the industries in Orissa declined towards the end of the 19th century. Till the beginning of the 19th century A.D, the ship building industry was more developed in Orissa than in England. Like the Orissan textile industry, it roused the jealousy of the english manufacturers and its progress and development were restricted by legislation.

To conclude the decline of these village based industries ultimately resulted in the growth of the poverty of the people. When the industries were closed the artisan engaged in those industries were thrown out of employment. These artisans tried to be accommodated in the only alternative that was agriculture. Agriculture could not absorb these categories of new wage earners. As a result of this poverty, they fled different places like Rangoon, Assam for livelihood. Thus, the decline of indigenous cottage industries had a serious impact on the economic growth of Orissa. Excepting noble attempts of Madhusudan Das, nothing significant attempt was taken by any individual or institution to promote handicrafts industries and save it from dying syndrome.

Madhusudan Das and Industrialisation of Orissa

Madhusudan Das had already emerged by the beginning of the 20th century as the indispensable leader of the Oriyas by organising the Oriya nationalism into a new form. His sympathy with the public cause and his pragmatic approach to many of the problems had already endeared him to the Oriyas who respectfully addressed him as the "Grand old man" even though he was only fifty.[102]

But this ambitious man was not happy with the small associations or their meetings which to him were not an end but only the means to bring about the progress and development of the Orissa. He started thinking deeply about the possibilities of the economic development in Orissa. In 1890, he established. "Orissa art wares" which he established with a view to expanding the cottage and the traditional small scale industries of Orissa.[103] He realised that in order to keep pace with time and to prosper, it would be wise to take greater interest in industry, Madhusudan Das is more often remembered for his contribution to Orissa's industrialisation. His attempts in this field were the more spectacular since no conscious efforts had been made in this direction.

Through the "Orissa art wares" he first started making on a large scale filigree works which are traditional handicrafts of Orissa. Various other cottage industries caught his attention too and he helped them develop on sounder footing. He exhorted the village weavers to come over to his workshop and receive better training in weaving.[104]

In 1905, he established the famous "Utkal tannery"- a shoe factory at Cuttack.[105] He was well aware of the importance of such a concern in view of the cheap export of huge quantities of raw leather to England and the subsequent selling of finished goods back in India at an exorbitant price.[106] Skins of crocodiles, serpents and lizards, which were easily available in Orissa, were collected for the shoe factory at his instance. Madhusudan laid utmost emphasis on the quality of the shoe that were being produced at his factory. Products used to be very meticulously examined for defects, and he was never prepared to compromise even with very minor imperfection. On account of this, the factory used to incur heavy losses at times but that could never force Madhusudan to deviate from his principle of putting reputation above everything else particularly when it came to the prestige of the Oriyas. "Utkal tannery" used to be frequently visited by important personalities all of whom were full of praise for it. Gopabandhu Das described this venture as a " Great deed".[107]

Unfortunately, however, inspite of the promise it showed, "Utkal tannery" became an increasingly losing concern and could not be sustained for long. It almost closed down in 1927.

It may be worthwhile to quote Swami Bichitrananda Das, who catalogues Madhusudan Das's contribution towards the industrialisation of Orissa.

"He emphasized the usefulness of cottage industry, the formation of joint stock companies and co-operative industries as early as 1903..... Really he lived much ahead of his time. He was 50 years ahead of his countrymen (in Orissa) but people did not take up the spirit of industrial life and did not like to develop the particular national genius of theirs but tried to seek jobs for making both ends meet. Even, so early in 1903 he introduced Charakha (spinning wheel) which was plied formerly in every house hold in Orissa. He helped and encouraged cotton cultivation to save the people from hard competition with west and to save the struggling weavers and cultivators in their hard competition with Manchester goods."[108]

FACTORIES AND MILLS

Aska sugar and rum factory

Except the sugar and rum factory at Aska, there was no other industry of note in this district. This factory was established in 1854. It was the first sugar factory of Asia.[109]

The factory at Aska was managed by a firm composed of european and native partners. The original value of the plant and machinery was estimated at Rs. 60,000, and the factory was furnished with machinery of the best construction driven by steam-power for the generation of which there was a large consumption of fuel.

The yearly out-turn of sugar from diffusion in 1880 was about 8,000 bags valued at Rs. 1,60,000. The factory turned out from cane 14 tones of sugar in 24 hours. 1,00,000 gallons of syrup was also manufactured yearly valued at Rs. 25,000.[110]

The jaggery, or sugar deprived of its syrups by the centrifugal process, was also largely manufactured. This phase of the sugar industry was however threatened with extinction on account of the unremunerative prices obtained in the raw sugar market at home, owing to the failure of sugar regaining as a trade, caused by the bounty on the export of refined sugar from France. The refining power of the Aska factory was equal to 2,000 tons of refined sugar of a value of Rs. 6,00,000. Since the demand for the jaggery of the Ganjam district for export was increasing, sugar refining had been almost abandoned in favour of diffusion after 1905.

The season of manufacture of sugar coincided with the cane season, i.e. from January to the end of March. The jurors of the Paris exhibition of 1878, granted a silver medal to Messrs Minchin & Co. of Aska for their excellent exhibits of crystal sugar.

The distillation of rum and other liquors was carried on in the most approved fashion and the liquors manufactured were much superior to those formerly distilled by the Oriya "Sundies", in whose hand the liquor traffic formerly lay. The rum was chiefly manufactured out of the Sugar molasses or syrup, which it was not found profitable to convert into sugar. For making country spirits, rice and mohwa flowers (Bassia latifolia) were principally used. Besides rum and country spirit, cognac and milk punch were manufactured. The factory also possessed one soda-water machine. The out-turn per year of rum was 1,50,000 gallons proof spirit. The distillery possessed two column stills, each capable of delivering from 1,000 to 1,200 gallons of proof spirit in 24 hours. The spirit reservoir lined with portland cement capacity of 16,000 gallons.[111]

The factory contained, besides the machinery and buildings connected with the manufacture of sugar and rum cooperate for making casks and a complete establishment for casting in iron and brass. In the busy season of the year it afforded employment to 1,000 men and women of whom 300 were mechanics, bricklayers, carpenters, stokers, engine man and man engaged in the foundry. During the idle months of the year 300 to 400 persons chiefly mechanics were employed.

The establishment of the Aska factory one of the biggest in India, had given not only a considerable stimulus to the cultivation of sugarcane, but at the same time had been the means of imparting to many of its inhabitants a skill as mechanics which they would have had no opportunities of acquiring elsewhere. It had thus indirectly borne no small share in the development of the district and its welfare.[112]

It is generally said that Orissa had never been an industrial state. But this is centrary to facts of history. Orissa arts and crafts had been the greatest contributor to the immense wealth of Orissa from time immemorial. The industrial commision report stated that even at a much later period when the merchant adventurers from the west made their first appearance in Orissa, the industrial development of this province was at any rate, not inferior to that of the more advanced european nations. By the first half of the 19th century, Orissa lost her supremacy in trade over the european world, which proud position she occupied for nearly two thousand years. She was now transformed into a country for production of raw materials and a market for dumping of cheap machine made goods produced in England.

The decay of the Orissan trade more or less complete by the middle of the 19th century. The causes of the decay may be summarised as (i) policy of the British parliament, (ii) competition of cheaper machine-made goods, (iii) lack of intention of the english government of India to protect and encourage Orissa arts and crafts, (iv) oppression of the Orissa manufactures, particularly the weavers by the company's servants, (v) according to some writers the industrial revolution in England and production of massive quantities of finished goods with the help of machinaries and consequently low cost of production enabled the english manufacturers to undersell the Indian manufacturers ; thus, raining the Orissa industries. But others are of the opinion that the very industrial revolution in England was "Consequence of the plundered wealth of India" and what the British did in Orissa was not to try to protect the Orissa industries but purposefully threw obstacles in their way and in certain cases discouraged Orissan manufacturers in order to help development of those in England. Steps were not taken to protect the Orissa industries, was not due to lack of statesmanship but due to the desire of the ruling authorities to promote the english industries at the cost of the Orissan. Thus, the main purpose of the trade of the english was exploitation of Orissan wealth.

Orissa was a self-sufficient unit so far her industrial requirements were concerned. There must have been an improvement in their economic conditions. The people of Orissa could produce all the necessary articles for life. Even, there were surplus productions of textile articles, oil, stone dishes, salt, etc. which could be exported to other parts of India and foreign countries. But the British administration throughout the 19th centrury did not encourage the people for the rapid growth of industries in Orissa. Rather, its policies were responsible for the decline of cottage industries. Except Aska Sugar factory, there was no big industries in Orissa. Madhusudan Das said that it was the divide and rule policy of the British administration that had suppressed the zeal of the Orissa artisans for the development of industries in Orissa. When industries decline the professional workers opt for agriculture. But shortage of agricultural lands rendered them unemployed. Orissa remained as an exporting land, rich with raw materials but no industrial development was made during the 19th century.

REFERENCES

1. A. Stirling, An account of Orissa proper or Cuttack, 1904, p.5.
2. S. C. Dey, History of the freedom movement of Orissa, p. 106.
3. B. C. Ray, Foundations of British Orissa, 1960, p. 204.
4. B. C. Roy, New lights on Maratha Orissa (Bhubaneswar, 1993), p. 228.
5. Calender of persion correspondence, Vol. IX, No. 605.
6. Krupasindhu Mishra, Utkala Itihasa, pp. 261-262.
7. Ibid.
8. W. Ewer, Correspondence of the settlements of Khoordah in Pooree (Reprinted in Orissa historical research journal), Vol. IV, No. 2, p. LXVI.
9. W. Ewer, op. cit, p. LXVI.
10. N. K. Sinha (E), Midnapur salt papers, pp. 1-4.
11. Ibid, pp. 4-6.
12. Calender of Persian correspondence, Vol. VI, No. 1242.
13. BJP (Cr) No. 26. of 5 September, 1805, Govt. to Commissioners of Cuttack.
14. C. Rundall, Report on the manufacture of salt and the system of administration of salt revenue of Balasore, Cuttack and Puri districts, 1883, Para-18.
15. Parliamentary papers 1856 H. C., Vol.26, Part-III, Bengal, (Report upon salt in British India) pp. 490-493, B. C. Ray, Foundation of British Orissa, 1960, p. 212.
16. Report on the administration of Bengal 1860-61 (Calcutta, 1861), p. 31.
17. Report as the administration of salt revenue in the Madras presidency, 1865-66, p. 131.
18. C. Rundall, op. cit, Para-18.

19. Report on the administration of Bengal, 1861-62, p. 17.
20. W. W. Hunter, History of Orissa, Vol. II. London, 1872, p. 486.
21. Report on the administration of salt department in the Bengal Presidency 1874-75, Para-4.
22. Report on the possibility of establishment of salt industry in coastal areas of Orissa, 1938, p. 11.
23. Annual general administration report of Orissa division, 1876-77, Para-25.
24. Narayan Rao, Growth of industries in the days of Madhusudan Das, "The journal of historical and social analysis", Vol. II, July-Dec. 1992, p. 42. Also B. S. Das, Studies in the economic history of Orissa, p. 270.
25. Report on the possibility of establishment of salt industry in coastal areas of Orissa, 1938, p. 11.
26. Ibid.
27. S. C. Agarwal, Salt industry in India, 1937, p. 161.
28. Ibid.
29. Fakir Mohan Senapati, Galpa Sulpa, p. 50.
30. Board of Revenue to Commissioner of Orissa, M. R. May, 1863, 8 April, 1863.
31. Dy. Commissioner, Salt and Abkari revenue, North division to Secy. to Commissioner, Salt, Abk and Salt revenue, Bengal, No. 746, 13 August 1887.
32. Ibid.
33. Report on the salt industry of Orissa, p. 12.
34. Ibid, p. 12.
35. Report on the possibility of Establishment of salt industry in coastal areas of Orissa, 1938, p. 34.
36. Ibid. p. 162.

37. Ibid. p. 13.
38. Ibid. p. 13.
39. Report on the salt industry of Orissa, p. 13.
40. Ibid, p. 13.
41. Fakir Mohan Senapati, Galpa Sulpa, p.50.
42. Ibid, p. 51.
43. M. R. (Deptt.), Dec. 1867 (11).
44. Laxmi Narayan Sahu, Anthology, p. 182.
45. Fakir Mohan Senapati, Galpa Salpa, p.126.
46. Ibid, p. 126.
47. L. N. Sahu, Anthology, p.124.
48. Kamala Devi Chattopadhyaya, "The glory of indian handicrafts, New Delhi, 1976, p. 7.
49. S. Sankaran, Economic development of India, Bombay, 1975 pp. 430-433
50. Bengal revenue proceedings, Customs, March 1818, C. Beeger, Collector of customs, Balasore to commissioner, Cuttack, March 2, 1818.
51. General administration report of Orissa division, 1880-81, p. 13.
52. Rai Bahadur B. C. Pattanaik, A Rough survey of the cottage industries of Orissa, p. 4.
53. BRP (Customs) March, 1818, C. Beager, Collector of customs, Balasore to commissioner, Cuttack, March 2, 1818.
54. General administration report of Orissa division 1880-81, p. 13, P. Mukherjee, History of Orissa, 1904, p. 430.
55. General administration report of Orissa division, 1880-81, p. 13.
56. A. P. Sha, Life in mediaeval Orissa (600 to 1200) Varanasi 1976, pp. 97-111.
57. Thomas Motte, "A narrative of journey to the diamond mines at Sambalpur", OHRJ, vol. I, No.3, October 1952, Appendix, II, pp. 1-49.
58. B. S. Das, Studies in economic history of Orissa from ancient times to 1833, Calcutta, 1978,

p. 210.

59. OHRJ, vol. I, July 1980, No. 2, pp. 56-59, K. M. Metter, A few notes in cotton stuff in the district of Cuttack, Calcutta 1897, pp.3-5.
60. N. K. Das, Madhusudan's immortal works, pp. 3-4.
61. Report on the progress of education in Orissa division for the quinquennium, 31 March, 1907, para-4.
62. Ibid, para-148.
63. Rai Bahadur B. C. Pattanaik, op. cit. p. 3.
64. L.S.S.O.' Malley, Bihar and Orissa Gazetteer, Cuttack, p. 152.
65. P. Mukherjee, History of Orissa,1904, p. 480.
66. General administration report of Orissa division (1899-1910), p. 9.
67. Ibid (1890-91), p. 8.
68. Ibid (1889-90), p. 9.
69. OHRJ, Vol. XXXIV, No. 384, Bhubaneswar, 1959, pp. 174-175.
70. M. N. Upadhyaya, Handicrafts of India, p. 40.
71. L.S.S.O' Malley, Bihar and Orissa gazetteers, Cuttack, p. 150.
72. File No. 126, Misc. Collection IV, 13 BRP, No. 38-46, May, 1890.
73. OHRJ, Vol. XXXIV, No. 384, p. 174-180.
74. Utkal Dipika, 17.11.1900.
75. OHRJ, Vol. XXXIV, No. 384, p. 180.
76. OHRJ, Vol. XXXIV, No. 384, p. 172.
77. M. N. Upadhyaya, op. cit, pp. 40-48.
78. B. C. Mohanty, Applique craft of Orissa, p. 56.
79. L.S.S.O' Malley, Bihar and Orissa gazetteers, Puri, p. 208.
80. Ibid.
81. Annual report of the Director of industries, Govt. of Bihar and Orissa for the year 1924-25, pp. 131-135.

82. S. K. Apata, British economic policy in south Orissa, 1858-1936, Unpublished, Ph. D thesis, Berhampur University, 1989, p. 257.
83. Annual report of the Director of industries, Bihar and Orissa for the year 1920-21, pp. 161-163.
84. H. B. Mohanty, op. cit, p. 53.
85. H. B. Mohanty, op. cit, p. 54.
86. Annual report of the Director of industries, Orissa, 1940-41, pp. 139-140.
87. Ibid.
88. B. C. H. R. Macfersion, Collector of customs Grey, Asst. collector of customs, False point, no. 21, July, 9, 1870 (OSA).
89. GAROD, 1876-77 and 1877-78.
90. R. C. Dutta, Economic history of India, Vol. II, p. 253.
91. General administration report of Orissa division, 1899-1900, p. 10.
92. Ibid.
93. Bipin Chandra, The rise and growth of economic nationalism in India (1880-1905), New Delhi, 1966, p. 55.
94. Utkal Dipika 14.11.1900, Orissa history congress proceedings of the XV annual session, p. 210.
95. R. Ker, Magistrate to Board of revenue, Sept. 1, 1806 (OSA).
96. S. M. Mishra, Economic troubles of Orissa, Vol. I, p. 379.
97. General administration report of Orissa division, 1890-1900, p. 31.
98. C. R. Wilson, Early annals of english in Bengal, Vol. II, Part-I, No. 1014.
99. B. C. Ray, Foundations of British Orissa, 1960, pp. 189-190.
100. Harcourt to Mr. Shaw, Private secretary to Governor General, august 9, 1804, MSS No.

1361, p. 33, Quoted by B. C. Ray foundations of British Orissa, 1960, p. 190.

101. G. Toynbee, A sketch of the history of Orissa, 1873, p. 193.
102. Utkal Dipika, 2.7.1898.
103. Ibid, 17.11.1900.
104. S. N. Das, Desaprana Madhusudan (Oriya) Cuttack, p. 227.
105. Ibid, p. 230.
106. Ibid, p. 232.
107. The Samaj (Oriya daily), 2.8.1924.
108. N. K. Das, Madhusudan's immortal works, pp. 3-4.
109. Dainik Asha (Oriya daily), 11.2.1882.
110. Ibid.
111. Asha, 30 August, 1921.
112. S. Mohanty, Madhusudan Das, p. 159.

Chapter - 6

IMPORT AND EXPORT DUTIES

There was a good state of commercial activity in Orissa by the beginning of the 19th century. Regulated markets, internal communications, investment capacity of the people, media of transactions and duties imposed by the government on articles play dominant roles in the growth of commercial activities of a community, so also a province. Orissa offered a unique position geographically and was a very suitable site for exchange. Import and export duties formed an important aspect in the history of trade of Orissa during the colonial era. Further, the manufacture of excisable articles like opium, liquor and ganja occupied an important role to play in the economic life of the people. After land revenue, the Britishers took keen interest in the subject and tried to develop it as a good source of revenue collection.

The Marathas, it appears, did not give any attention to the collection of custom duties[1] although they exported 3 lakh maunds of salt Berar[2] and 68 thousand maunds (at the average) of salt to Calcutta per annum.[3] But as a trading race, the British intended to collect as much money as possible either in the way of revenue (taxes) or as customs. Therefore, they devised the system of custom duties.

The customs consisted partly of an inland transit duties levied on the import and export trade of the province. For an analytical study the discussion in this chapter may be categorised into the following heads :

(A) INLAND TRANSIT DUTIES

Duties on inland transit or trade may be broadly classified into two heads such as :

(i) Duties on excisable articles, and

(ii) Duties on non-excisable articles.

The greater portion of the duties was collected in transit of goods at the inland chowkeys. It was evident from the fact that out of the total collections of Rs. 60,679.5 annas from 1835 to 1839 only, Rs. 4,937.8 annas were collected at the sea ports (custom houses) and the rest of the amount was collected as the inland transit duties.[4]

(i) Duties on excisable articles

The Marathas derived no revenues or duties from excisable articles such as *opium, liquor, ganja, bhang,* etc. In Orissa, liquors were manufactured and opium was sold without any restriction in the province.[5] But the British government took of the matter immediately after their conquest and in course of time the revenue derived from excisable articles became one of the main source of income.

The British government established a separate department known as *"Abkari"* for the collection of excise duties in the very beginning of their administration in Orissa. In 1805, the commissioner for the affairs of Cuttack reported that the average receipts in the department of *"Abkari"* for a period of 6 months had been sicca Rs. 936 and the expense was sicca Rs. 182 per month.[6] Perhaps it was on account of such a small profit, the government neglected it for a number of years. The supervision of this branch of revenue at first was vested with the Board of Revenue, but in 1819 it was transferred to the newly established Board of Customs, Salt and Opium.[7]

Duties on Spirit

There were two systems under which the excise revenue of Orissa was raised by the British. They were known as monthly tax system and the fixed duty system. Both systems were adopted in case of country liquor but in case of other excisable articles, fixed duty system was adopted. The principle of fixed duty system was the levy of duty on the actual quantity of spirit of drug which passed into consumption.[8]

The regulation 10 of 1813 formed the basis of future *"Abkari"* administration in Orissa. According to this regulation the first public distillery was established at Cuttack in 1814 at an expense of 800 rupees. Three kinds of spurious liquors were prepared at this distillery, such as liquor from sugar or molasses, liquor from grain, generally rice and liquor from the mowah flowers. The cost of manufacture of the first kind of liquor was about 7 annas per gallon and it was sold about 14 annas. The other two kinds of inferior liquors cost from 2 annas to 5 annas and they were sold from 4 annas to 12 annas per gallon. The retail liquor shops paid duty of 6 annas per day in

1814.[9] But the "Tari" (prepared from plam tree) sellers paid 4 annas per shop.

Introduction of Madras contract distillery system

In 1805 a great change was introduced in the administration of country spirit revenue of Orissa. With a view to improve the system of excise, Madras contract distillery system was introduced in Orissa. In consequence, distillers were converted into warehouses for the storage of liquor. The local manufacture of country spirit was absolutely forbidden and the contract for the wholesale supply of spirit was given to Messers Crew & Co. of the Resa distillery in the united provinces. The liquor was generally brought from the Resa distillery into Midnapur warehouse and was then transported to Orissa. The duty fixed for the liquor supplied under the contract system was the same as under the old distillery system i.e. Rs. 3/- per gallon.[10]

There was a substantial increase of revenue from the country spirit. However, the increase was not as marked in the case of ganja and opium. The people of Orissa drank little. They however made up their abstinence from spirit by excessive indulgence in opium and ganja.[11] In that context L.S.S.O. 'Malley wrote, "The fact is that, the Oriya, is far from being a hard drinker and the demand for liquor is so slight that it is found sufficient to have one retail shop for every 71, 413 persons."[12]

Duties on Ganja

Another excisable articles which fetched much duties to the government was ganja. The ganja was the male plant of the hemp. The ganja consumed in Orissa were of two kinds such as Rajshahi ganja and Garhjat ganja. The Rajshahi ganja was extensively cultivated in the tract of land lying in the Rajshahi district in the province of Bihar. The Garhjat ganja was produced in the Garhjats or Tributary states of Orissa. The Garhjat ganja was much inferior in narcotic power to that grown in Rajshahi. The Rajshahi ganja was of three varieties, flat, round and char. The round form of Rajshahi ganja, was mostly consumed in Orissa. The duty on flat ganja, round ganja and char ganja in 1864 was Rs. 2, Rs. 3 and Rs. 4 respectively, In 1877 the duty of flat and round ganja was raised to Rs. 3.8.0 and Rs. 9 respectively. The ganja was doubtless the most injurious of all the articles which contributed to the excise revenue. There the main object of the enhancement of duty was to check the immediate consumption and at the same time to augment the public revenue."[13]

The Garhjat ganja was extensively smuggled into Orissa because of its low price and low duty. With a view to putting a check on the smuggling, the duty on imported Garhjat ganja was raised to Rs. 4 seer in 1878. In a maximum of revenue from a minimum of consumption in the taxation of excisable articles, the duty on ganja was raised from time to time. It was raised to Rs. 6.8.0 annas, Rs. 6 and Rs.4-8-0 annas on chur, round and flat ganja respectively from March 22, 1893 and was again raised to Rs. 7-8-0 annas, Rs. 6-4-0 annas and Rs. 4-8-0 annas respectively from 1 January, 1894. Inspite of that, the rates were kept much lower than in the rest of the Bengal presidency with in view to reduce temptation to smuggling from the adjacent Tributary mahals.[14]

From 23 May, 1905, a uniform rate of duty was fixed on all description of ganja, whether chur, round or flat at the rate of Rs. 9 per seer. The duties derived from ganja was in steady increase year after year.[15]

Duties on Bhang, Churs

Bhang or Siddhi and Churs were the preparations of ganja-bhang was an intoxicating drink prepared from larger leaves and capsules. Churs was the resin of the plant extracted while it was growing.

Bhang was prepared for domestic use in several parts of Orissa. But it was brought for wholesale vend chiefly from Mungher and Bhagalpur. It was stored and retailed in the same way as ganja-churs was obtained from north-western provinces and Nepal under a pass from the collector of the district in which it was to be sold by the importer. The duty on Bhang was fixed at the rate of 8 annas a seer in addition to licence fees. In October 1880 the duty on Churs was fixed at the rate of Rs. 8 per a sheer.[16]

Duties on Opium

The duties from opium alone consituted two third of the duties levied on all excisable articles. With regard to the increasing consumption of opium. Jones, the collector of Cuttack remarked, " The people of Orissa were notoriously addicted to this drug. From the highest to the lowest caste and without distinction of age and creed, the drug was taken freely by the people. Caste rules exercised no deterrent influence to check the progress of consumption as they do in the case of spirits. On the other hand, an impression generally prevails that, the use of opium has a solutary affect on the health of its consumers, especially during old age. So long as the idea exists in the minds of the people, the revenue derived from the opium will always done."[17] The government had a monopoly of the manufacture and sale of opium. It was grown in the Bihar districts, only. The drug was prepared at the Bihar government agency and sent to the collectors of all districts for sale to the public at fixed prices. The opium was issued at these prices to retail vendors from every district and sub-divisional treasury.[18]

The price of the opium had been raised from time to time to check the increasing consumption of the drug. In 1860 the price of opium was raised from Rs. 16 to Rs. 22 per seer.[19] It was again raised to Rs. 25 in 1873. The duty of one rupee was levied on every opium licences per one seer with effect from 1 April 1870,[20] which resulted in the increase of revenues.

Duties on Rum

Rum is the spirit manufactured in India on english method. The duty levied on Rum was Rs. 3 per gallon.[21] In 1880 the source of supply of rum in Orissa changed from Calcutta to Aska in Ganjam.[22] In 1880 Messers Minchin & Co. manufacturers of rum at Aska applied for permission to sell liquor in Orissa, on payment of duty at one rupee per gallon.[23] In 1883 the duty was raised to Rs. 2 per gallon.

In 1887 the duty on rum was raised to Rs. 5 per gallon. This was again raised to Rs. 6 per gallon with effect from 10 January 1898. But the enhancement of the duty had no effect on revenue as the rum was little consumed by the people of Orissa. Therefore the revenue from rum fluctuated between Rs. 1,000 and Rs. 2,500 per year.[24]

Before the British occupation spurious liquors were manufactured and opium was sold without any restrictions in the province. The British government took notice of it and decided to impose taxes on such excisable articles. The management and collection of the "Abkari" revenue was placed in the hands of the collector of land revenue. The government did not take part in the manufacture of excisable articles such as spurious liquor, opium, ganja, rum, etc., but it gave licence to certain persons to open shops for sale at a fixed rate of tax. But the government failed to check the manufacture of illicit liquor, tari and illicit plantation of ganja. This system continued till 1828 and the government revenue realised from "Abkari" articles was slowly increased as per the following statistics.

1808-09	-	Sicca	Rs.	9,123
1809-10	-	Sicca	Rs.	9,582
1810-11	-	Sicca	Rs.	9,644
1814-15	-	Sicca	Rs.	15,000
1824-25	-	Sicca	Rs.	40,793
1827-28	-	Sicca	Rs.	42,176[25]

Due to the steady increase of "Abkari" revenue, the government became more interested to bring changes in the management of "Abkari" department. Three posts of collector, Cuttack, Puri, Balasore remained under the control of the commissioner from March 1829 subject to the further control of the Board of Customs, Salt and Opium. According to the new system, the vendors were asked to pay their dues not in a uniform rate as before but in the rate as fixed by the collector in first 6 months during which period, there was maximum demand. The rate of opium also increased from sicca Rs. 21-11-9 pies to Rs. 25-8 annas per seer. Out of this amount sicca Rs. 5 was credited to the opium department as the cost of production and the balance of sicca Rs. 20 was credited to the Abkari department as Abkari revenue.[26] Further, the price of opium was raised to Rs. 30-13 annas.[27] The following table shows the detail statistics of Abkari revenue.

	1837-38		1838-39	
Name of the articles	**No. of shops**	**Amount realised Rs. P.**	**No. of shops**	**Amount Realised Rs. P.**
CUTTACK				
Opium	1	8,428-1-2	1	7,438-0-0
Liquor	18	2,221-8-6	15	2,674-2-03
Tari	150	2,163-10-7	138	1883-14-01
Ganja	1	3,102-8-0	1	2,737-8-0
Total		**15,995-12-3**		**14,733-8-4**
BALASORE				
Opium	2	13,456-14-8	1	12,648-0-0
Liquor	6	556-6-5	6	595-0-5
Tari	4	841-14-6	4	771-13-2
Ganja	22	463-12-10	22	471-7-4
Total		**15,319-0-5**		**14,486-4-11**
PURI				
Opium	6	1169-0-0	6	2,325-0-0
Liquor	31	1382-7-5$\frac{1}{4}$	21	1,968-13-2$\frac{1}{4}$
Tari	50	1017-15-3$\frac{1}{4}$	50	1,017-15-3$\frac{1}{4}$
Ganja	7	1043-10-0	—	—
Total		**4,613-0-8$\frac{1}{2}$**		**5,311-12-5$\frac{1}{2}$**

A new system was introduced on August, 1847[28] and accordingly, two Abkari superintendents were appointed to be remained under the control of the commissioner. One remained in charge of both Cuttack and Puri district. Cuttack was divided into five divisions, Balasore into four and Puri into three. An elaborate and efficient administrative system was promulgated for the collection of "Abkari" revenue. The statistics submitted to the board of revenue revealed that the "Abkari" revenue collection increased in subsequent years.

1852-53	-	Rs.	60,944
1954-55	-	Rs.	62,725
1855-56	-	Rs.	77,663
1856-57	-	Rs.	83,742
1857-58	-	Rs.	93,667
1873-74	-	Rs.	2,97,786
1876-77	-	Rs.	3,10,469
1878-79	-	Rs.	3,78,592[29]

Government did not like to make any changes in the existing partice due to the appearance of Orissa famine except in the matter of the illicit importation of Garhjat ganja into the regulated districts of Orissa. Bengal Act VII of 1878 was promulgated and extended to Orissa.[30] According to the provisions the administration of excise department was reorganised. A commissioner was appointed to look into the administration separately. The act provided for the establishment of a Sadar distillery in each district. The act also provided certain preventive measures to check the illicit importation of Garhjat ganja which resulted in the steady increase of Abkari revenue in succeeding years. The table shows the example :-

1880-81	-	Rs.	4,09,690
1881-82	-	Rs.	4,59,826
1882-83	-	Rs.	4,63,683
1885-86	-	Rs.	5,03,298
1888-89	-	Rs.	5,22,438
1892-93	-	Rs.	5,60,977
1893-94	-	Rs.	6,10,535
1897-98	-	Rs.	6,62,775
1898-99	-	Rs.	7,27,438
1899-1900	-	Rs.	7,34,098[31]

The total number of shops of all kinds in the year 1899-1900 was 943 against during 2 years 1895-96 and 1896-97 was nearly the same being 891 but there was small but steady increase in the number since 1897-98[32]. The opening of more shops in Orissa to retail the excisable articles was felt. The increase of "Abkari" revenue was very high. The commissioner, attributed the cause of this increase to be influx of people for railway work in Bengal-Nagpur railway.

Thus, a new source of revenue was tapped by the British authorities and inspite of several experiments, the revenue was steadily increasing. The excise revenue was a very important source of revenue in the province and it had increased rapidly and reached a new height by the end of the 19th century.

(ii) Duties on non-excisable articles

Besides the duties on excisable articles, the government also levied duties on non-excisable articles like salt, cotton, rice and jungle products during their inland transit. Among the non-excisable articles, the salt monopoly in Orissa yielded much profit to the company's government. According to Andrew Stirling, the finest salt of all India was manufactured in the coastal region of Orissa and it gave annually to the company a net revenue falling short of 18 lakhs of rupees. In course of time the net profit from the salt monopoly soared very high. The revenue derived from the salt monopoly in Orissa both from local sale in the province and public sale at Sulkia was about 39 lakhs of rupees towards the end of the company's rule. It was more than the double of the land revenue of the province which was about 17 lakhs of rupees after the long term settlement of 1837. Thus, the salt monopoly was the principal source of revenue to the British government in Orissa. In fact, it formed the second principal source of revenue to the company's government in Bengal. The net annual receipt from it often exceeding a crore of rupees and sometimes even amounting to one crore and a half.[33] Salt monopoly was, "entirely the creation of the British government" but perhaps no other source of revenue was so entirely based on narrow commercial outlook of the company.

During the company's administration, government collected Rs. 2.8 annas as duty on salt per maund.[35] This fell, heavily upon the consumable. Inspite of the evil pointed out by George Plowden the said duty was enhanced to Rs. 3 in 1859 and Rs. 3-4 annas in 1860.[36] However the duty on Ganjam (south Orissa) salt was Rs. 1.5 annas per mound. The question of the difference of duty levied on salt in north

Orissa & Ganjam (south Orissa) respectively, which effected prejudicially in the sales in south Orissa and more especially those of Puri district formed a subject of lengthy correspondence between the Government of Bengal and India, and the Government of Madras and India.[36]

As the best means of protecting the salt revenue of Orissa, the Lieutenant Governor of Bengal recommended the Government of India : "The duty on Ganjam salt should be raised to an equality with that of Orissa, and failing this the Madras government be absolutely prohibited from granting passes for salt into the province of Orissa or the Tributary mahals."[37]

But the Government of Madras strongly opposed this proposal. Against the opposition of the Government of Madras the question was finally disposed of by the Government of India in September, 1863. It was decided that the full Bengal duty of Rs. 3-4 annas was to be levied by the collector of Ganjam on all Ganjam salt introduced for exportation into Bengal and the difference between that duly and the lower Madras duty, Rs. 1-6 annas was to be credited to the Government of Bengal.[38] But large quantities of Madras Salt, on which differential duty has not been found their way into the Tributary mahals, Sambalpur and central provinces from Ganjam. This led to the introduction of the graduated scale of duty in Orissa to connect the low Madras duty with the higher duty of Orissa. Moreover, the selling price of salt in Ganjam was raised from Rs. 2 to Rs. 2-4 annas.[39]

For introducing the graduated scale of duty, Orissa was divided into six zones with different rate of duty for each. They were fixed by the Government of India in April, 1874.[40]

The effect of the graduated scale of duty on the local trade was very serious. It stimulated the imports of Ganjam salt into Orissa. In 1877 the duty on Ganjam salt was raised to Rs. 2.1 annas.[41] In July 1878, the rates of duty on salt manufactured in Orissa were revised and reduced to the scale of Rs. 2-8 annas for the whole of the district of Puri and Cuttack Rs. 2-10 annas for the portion of Balasore district lying between Cuttack and Kansbans river and Rs. 2-12 annas for the rest of the district.[42] The duty on salt was further reduced and a uniform rate of Rs. 2 was levied throughout Orissa from March, 1882.[43] In 1905 there was a further reduction of duty on salt to Rs. 1-8 annas. This rate of duty remained unchanged throughout the rest of the period under review.

No duty was levied on grain or food stuffs. However, the Rajas and Zamindars of Orissa used to levy duties called "Sayar" upon every articles of commerce and necessities of life, either in the course of their transit from one place to another or at the places of their sale. This duty was collected at chowkey or custom stations situated at the strategic places of their states.[44]

(B) DUTIES ON OVER-SEAS TRADE

In ancient times Orissa was a seafaring country and her maritime activities resulted in establishment of colonies in the Indian archipelago. But when the two european travellers, Thomas Motte and Leckie, passed through Orissa in the second half of the 18th century did not find its commercial prosperity at all. In 1766 Thomas

Motte was sent on a mission to Sambalpur by Lord Clive. He started from Calcutta and passed Balasore and Cuttack towards his destination and also returned through the same route. His "Narrative of a journey to the diamond mines of Sambalpur" is rather silent about the trade and commerce of the provinces.[45] In 1790 Lord Cornwallis deputed George Forester on a mission to Nagpur. His party started from Calcutta on March 7, 1790 and passed through Balasore and Cuttack towards Nagpur. It included Leckie who kept an account of the journey, and that was published by his brother G.F. Leckie in April 1880. Leckie described "Balasore was formerly a flourishing port, but their manufacture of the sanoes clothes is very much fallen off, both in quality and quantity; and the ruinous state of the English and Dutch factors, with the insignificance of the Danish one, seem to show that the trade is not of that consequence which it formerly was."[46] From the above description it is evident that, the commercial prosperity of the province had gradually dwindled and by the end of the 18th century it was at its lowest ebb.[47]

However, soon after the British occupation of Orissa, the Governor-General in council passed certain rules for the management of the department of customs in Orissa.[48] The customs consisted partly of duties levied on the import and export trade of the country and partly of an inland transit duty.

(1) Export and import duties during the company's period

According to the rules passed on May 4, 1804, only a single duty was to be imposed on the import of goods from any foreign country either by sea or land. After the payment of that duty, the merchant might carry his goods to whatever part of the province he felt most conducive to his own interest without any interference on part of government officers.[49]

Goods of every description, except a few articles on being imported by sea from Bengal or any other part of the British possessions in India, accompanied with a "rowanah" were required to pay a duty of $2\frac{1}{2}\%$ on the valuation specified there in. Goods of every description, except a few article, on being imported or exported by sea or by land and not accompanied with a "rowanah", were required to pay the duty on every kind of goods as specified in the book of rates.

The following articles were exempted from duty on being imported or exported either by sea or land. But it was required that the quantity or number and value must be specified to the darogah of the "chowkeys" through which the same might pass. The articles were.[50]

1. Wheat, rice and grain of every description.
2. Gold and silver bullion either coined or uncoined.
3. Timber or wood usually employed for ship or boat building, household or other purposes.
4. Pearls, diamonds or other precious stones.
5. Opium purchased at the company's sales at Fort William.
6. Hackeries and carriages of every description.
7. Image intended for religious purposes of every kind.

8. Instruments of agriculture or manufacture, ploughs tools and every articles of that description.

Except of salt petre from the province by sea or land was strictly prohibited. So also export of salt by sea was strictly prohibited except on account of the government or on the production of a "rowanah" for small quantities for the use of the ships, or boats, crew. The import or export of canon, gun powder and war like instruments or store into it from the province by land or sea was strictly prohibited,[51] or land would be subject to confiscation. One fourth of the value or the confiscated goods was to be paid to the informer and one fourth to the darogah or the "chowkey" by whose vigilance the seizure might have been made. Darogahs and all other officers employed in the department of customs were prohibited from taking or receiving any allowance either in money or in kind under any pretence whatever from any merchant. If any one of them disobeyed the rules, he was required to pay four times the amount so received besides being dismissed from his office.[52]

In the meantime all kinds of "sayar" duties were abolished by the regulation 12 of 1805 and on inland transit duty was substituted for the abolished "sayar". The import and export duties were regulated from England on the principle, of course, of favouring British manufacturers as much as possible. The transit duties were levied on all goods, manufactured in the country or imported by land in the British possessions. The goods were made to pay a separate duty at each of the custom house they passed. So when they reached the consumer, they were taxed with single, double or tripple duties according to the length of the journey,. In 1810 this system was abolished by a new regulation.[53]

On April 10, 1810 the new regulation was passed for rescinding all regulations in force for collection of government customs in the provinces of Bengal, Bihar and Orissa and for re-establishing those duties with amended rules for their collection. The custom house for the collection of government customs under this regulation was established in the town of Balasore for Orissa. It remained in charge of collector of government customs, and he was subject to the authority of the Board of Revenue at the presidency. The regulation also enumerated the rates of duty to be levied on different articles and enlisted the articles which were to be exempted from the payment of such duties. It declared that the goods which paid the duty once should not be liable to payment of any other duty. Of course, the "rowanahs" were to remain in force for one year only.[54]

Besides the central customs house at Balasore, 8 custom "chowkeys" were established at different places around it. They were :

NAME OF CHOWKEY	***DISTANCE FROM BALASORE***
Baliapal	12 coss (24 miles)
Rajghat	12 coss (24 miles)
Remuna	3 coss (6 miles)
Balaramhgari	3 coss (6 miles)
Fulwar	$\frac{1}{2}$ coss (1 mile)
Bangreah	$\frac{1}{2}$ coss (1 mile)
Chudamani	1-2 coss (24 mile)
Dhamrah	24 coss (48 miles)[55]

The above noted "chowkeys" were all situated in the district of Balasore and stretched from river Dhamra in south to river Subarnarekha in north. The custom house was established in the principal port of the province at Balasore. No doubt there were a number of smaller ports along the coastal like of Orissa from the river Dhamra in north to the Chilka lake in south. But perhaps the maximum volume of trade passed through the principal port at Balasore and other smaller ports of the district. So the government established the custom house and the "chowkeys" in that district only. No provision was made for the collection of customs in the district of Puri in the south.[56]

In 1820 certain rules were adopted by the government to be observed by the collectors of customs in transit of public stores belonging to His Majesty's government or to the company. The collector of customs at Balasore was accordingly directed to give effect to the arrangements. It was provided that such goods when imported should be entered in a separate import duty or free sea register which was to be kept at the custom house. As regards the export of goods by the government, an application was to be made to the collector of customs in the same form used by the indian merchants. The application was to specify the quantity and value of the goods, the number and description of the package and the places from where they came. On receipt of such an application, the collector of customs was required to depute an officer to be present at the loading of the same for shipment. That officer was to see that no more goods were sent than the quantity specified in the application. An entry of every such export of goods was to be made afterwards at the custom house in a separate "Free Export Register" to be maintained for such purposes.[57]

It specifically declared that military and medical stores and generally all articles belonging to the government in its territorial capacity should be exempted from the payment of duty on import, export or transit,. But in all instances applications, officially attested should be sent to pass such stores by the public officer in the department from which they were to be issued. They must certify them to be the property of the government and should give the identity of the person for whom they might be intended.[58]

In 1821 the Governor-General in council passed a resolution in modification of the system under which goods not exceeding 10 rupees in value were permitted to pass. The collector of customs at Balasore was directed to give effect to the modified rules. It was resolved that persons, passing through the outer range of "chowkeys" attached to any custom house, and not entering the city or town at which the collector of customs was stationed, should be allowed to carry with them any goods belonging to them without being subject to the payment of any transit duty. But the value of such goods should be less than 10 rupees and the weight of which might not exceed one maund of the local standard. The resolution was a laudable measure to help the common people who were subjected to the payment of transit duty in carrying small things within the jurisdiction of custom "chowkeys". Besides the provisions made by the above noted resolution, only a few articles produced in the country were allowed to pass free of duty such as grain, fire wood, ghee and a few petty goods.[59]

The net collections from the customs duties in Orissa were as follows :-

1816-17	Rs. 18,852	-	9	annas
1817-18	Rs. 23,294	-	7	annas
1818-19	Rs. 15,361	-	6	annas
1819-21	Rs. 20,611	-	13	annas
1821-22	Rs. 14,486	-	14	annas
1822-23	Rs. 16,425	-	0	annas[60]

In subsequent years, the net collections rapidly declined. From the statement of the collections for four years from 1825-26 to 1828-29 it was found that the total amount collected, during the period were Rs. 60,670.5 annas and the total expenses incurred, Rs. 25,301.3 annas. Thus the net process was during those years amounted to Rs. 35,369.2 annas, making an average of Rs. 8,842.4 annas only per year.[61]

The main cause of decrease in the collection of duties was the gradual decline of the volume of trade that passed through the Balasore custom house. In 1825 the collector of customs reported to the board that the decline was mainly perceptible in the trade of cotton goods. He pointed out that large quantities of cotton goods were manufactured in Cuttack and generally passed through Balasore customs house towards Calcutta for sale. The quantity manufactured in 1825 had been less in consequence of disputes between the principal cloth merchants of the province and their agents at Calcutta. Also a portion of the actual quantity produced found its way to Tributary mahals without coming within the limits of the government "chowkeys". The merchants further noticed that large quantities of cloth were being imported from Europe and sold at cheap rates in the market. The people generally preferred cheap foreign goods to costly indigenous products.[62]

In this connection Andrew Stirling, a British officer who had served in Orissa, wrote in 1825 "The manufactures and trade of Orissa proper are very inconsiderable and unimportant. A sufficiency of the coarser cloths is made for the use of the inhabitants in all parts of the district. The calicoes of Balasore, Soro, Badrak, Janjipur and Hariharpur were once much prized and sought after under the name of Sannahs, but the demand for the finer fabrics of that description having long since greatly decline, the quantity now manufactured is very trifling." In November, 1817 the collector of government customs at Balasore also observed that" the trade here is so trifling and the merchants and people in general so poor that few if any articles of the quality are ever brought here for sale."[63]

Although the number of small trading vessels which belonged to the port of Balasore, Chudamani and Dhamrah was considerable yet the export was almost entirely confined to grain on which no duty was levied. Naturally the collection of duties in the sea ports was small. Henry Rickets, the collector of government customs at Balasore, reported to the board in August 1829 that the collections on account of export and import for four years from May 1825 to April 1829 at Balasore averaged only Rs. 376.2 annas per annum, at Dhamra Rs. 431.7 annas per annum, at Chudamani Rs. 105.3 annas per annum and at Baliapal on river Subarnarekha Rs. 322.8 annas per annum. He pointed out that the revenue was so small as to claim little attention except as to how it could be realized at the least practicable expenses. In this connection the propriety of introducing the system of farming the collection of customs was raised. Rickets was of the opinion that the farming system would avoid unnecessary delay in removing goods in the small ports away from Balasore.[64]

However, the small income of the custom house prompted other officers in its charge to make fresh suggestions. In November 1833 Robert Hunter, the commissioner of Cuttack recommended to the government to abolish the Balasore custom house altogether. He pointed out that the trade was very small and much of the duties collected at Balasore would doubtless be collected at the Calcutta customs house if the former was abolished. The pecuniary loss to the government would be insignificant but the constant irritation of merchants for unavoidable delay in examining the goods and granting "rowanahs" would be got rid of.[65] On February 1, 1836 the collector of customs at Balasore also raised the question of abolishing the custom house and requested the commissioner to take up the question seriously. He declared that the profit to the government from the custom house was from 5 to 6 thousand rupees but "I think the annoyance caused by the custom house to the inhabitant may be reckoned at about 50,000". Henry Ricketts, the then commissioner of Cuttack, reported to the board in February, 1836 that the custom house which yielded only a profit of Rs. 8,000 per annum the prosperity of its being abolished could hardly be questioned. But the government was not prepared to take such a drastic step in abolishing the custom house altogether.[66]

How meagre was the collection from export and import duties in the Balasore custom house is shown in the following statements.

Year	Export Rs. As	Import Rs. As	Total Rs. As
1832-33	5.0	249.2	254.2
1833-34	-	157.8	157.8
1834-35	-	69.6	69.6[67]
Total	5.0	476.0	481.0

Rickets of course, did not suggest to make the port duty free because of his apprehension that such a measure might be injurious to the revenue derived from the custom house at Calcutta. At Dhamrah, Chudamani and Baliapal actually no trade was carried on but on the same principle that a check was to be maintained at Balasore, it might also be necessary to keep officers at those stations.[70]

The board agreed with the views of the commissioner. They also apprehended that if the ports under the Balasore customhouse were to be declared free, merchants from other parts of presidency would take advantage of the situation and utilize the free ports for export and import of their goods to avoid the payment of customs duties. To obviate abuses, the board decided that the custom house at Balasore should be maintained but with much reduced establishment. Thus a revised system came to be enforced from April 1836.[71]

During this preiod, the main articles of export were as before, rice and paddy. The quantity exported varied considerable and was regulated by several factors. It mainly depended on the state of crops in the province and the demand for it in the neighbouring provinces. It also varied according to the number of ships employed in salt trade and the period of the year at which the salt export was completed. Because at the time only the vessels employed in salt trade were available for export of other articles. It is certain that the whole export trade derived its impetus from government monopoly of salt on its export in large quantities from Orissa.[72]

As the collector of customs reported to Henry Ricketts, the then member of the Board of Revenue, the number of vessels in the port of Balasore had increased from 56 in 1831 to 167 in 1853. There were 185 vessels engaged in trade in the port during 1851 but 44 vessels were lost in the cyclone of that year, the greater number of which were soon replaced by new and better vessels. The trade of the port was mainly carried with Calcutta but a few vessel also to other Indian ports like Madras, Masulipatam and Calcutta. The account of vessels which cleared out from the customhouse during 1849 and 1850 was as follows :

Year	*To what port bound*	*No. of vessels cleared out*	*No. of arrivals reported*	*No. of whose arrivals not reported*
1849	Calcutta	282	167	115
	Madras	8	6	2
	Masulipatam	2	-	2
1850	Calcutta	357	204	153
	Madras	23	12	11
	Calcutta	1	—	—
	Total	673	389	284[71]

The number of vessels whose arrivals in the ports of their destination were not reported, as shown above, was considerable, and it was a matter of surprise to the board. However, the collector of customs could not believe that there had been any evasion of duties and that those unreported vessels had at all been to foreign ports. He was informed that many of the small crafts that cleared out for Calcutta. Many of them remained in the neighbourhood of Calcutta and did not report themselves to the custom house.[72]

Besides the customs duties, another kind of duty was also levied in the sea ports of the Balasore district from 1846 on all vessels loaded with any other cargo than salt. It was known as "buoyage"s duty for buoys's were placed on the mouth of the river to show navigable course of reefs etc. The rates of buoyage duties were as follows :

Vessels below 2000 maunds	Rs. 8 each
Vessels from 2000 maunds to 5000 maunds	Rs. 10 each
Vessels above 5000 maunds	Rs. 15 each[73]

It had already been noticed that the Balasore customs house gave no profit to the government from 1836 when the transit duties were abolished. Perhaps after the introduction of buoyage duties, it produced a small annual income.[74]

Though buoy's were provided only on the mouths of the Balasore and Dhamra rivers, the buoyage duties were charged at other smaller ports of the district such as, Chudamani, Lychanpur, Channoah, Sartha and Subarnarekha. However when an act was passed in 1855 (act 22 to 1855) for the regulation of ports and ports dues by the

Government of India, the commissioner of Cuttack objected to the extension of the act to those small ports including Dhamrah.[75] The main objection was based on the insignificance of trade in those small ports. Balasore was the only port of some importance in the province. On enquiry, W. White, the officiating master attendant of Balasore, supplied the statements of the number of vessels which paid buoyage duties and the amount of such duties realized for 5 years 1852 to 1856. The statements were as follow :[76]

Export and import vessels levied buoyage duties from the several rivers of the district.

Year	Subarnarekha	Sartha	Balasore	Lochanpur	Chudamani	Dhamrah	Total Vessels
1852	2	22	64	20	14	38	160
1853	14	42	73	24	4	34	191
1854	10	46	72	12	6	56	202
1855	14	35	69	16	19	31	184
1856	15	37	107	21	39	8	227

PORT DUES REALISED

Year	Total No. of vessels	Port dues or buoyage duties in Rs.
1852	160	1,436/-
1853	191	1,667/-
1854	202	1,850/-
1855	184	1,701/-
1856	227	2,071/-

But, the Government of India did not agree with their proposal. In 1858 a new act was passed (Act II of 1858) "for the levy of port-dues in certain ports in the province of Cuttack."[77] Such ports were Balasore, Chudamani, Lochanpur, Channoah, Sartha, Subarnarekha and Dhamrah. In accordance with the new act, the port dues were to be realised from May 1, 1858, "at the rate of 6 annas for every one hundred maunds of burden in respect of every sea-going vessel of the burden of 300 maunds and upwards which shall enter any of the said port." The act further provided that" he said several ports shall be regarded as consituting a single port. All sums received on account of port dues at any of the said ports shall from a common fund which shall be called the Balasore port fund, and shall be available for the payment of all charges incurred on account of any of the said ports.[78]

Thus, by the end of the East India company's rule, Balasore and other small ports in the district stretching from river Subarnarekha in the north and river Dhamra in south were brought under the regulations of the government. Though trade and commerce of the province had already dwindled and the fame of Balasore as a great sea port had faded away, yet the halo was somewhat maintained by the British government. The custom house for the province was located at Balasore, and it was still the principal port of the province. The other small ports of the district also attracted the attention of the government, and they were brought under the jurisdiction of the port act. But it was strange that, the government had no provision for the collection of customs in the district of Cuttack and Puri were brought under the said act. Obviously, the largest volume of trade passed through the ports and custom house of Balasore.

(ii) Export and import duties of Orissa under the British crown

At the time of the transfer of administration of India from the East India Company to the crown, import duties in India consisted of a $3\frac{1}{2}$ percent duty on cotton twist in a year, and a 5 per cent duty on other British goods, including cotton piece-goods. The rate of duty on goods from other foreign countries was double of this. The financial difficulties of the Government of India emanating from revolt of 1857 forced it in 1859 to raise the import tariff on cotton twist and yarns of 5 per-cent and 10 percent on other articles. In the following year the duty on cotton twist and yarn was also increased to 10 percent. But under pressure from British traders and cotton manufacturers, a process of tariff reform and reduction, particularly on cotton products, was soon set in motion. The duty on cotton piece-goods was cut down to 5 percent in 1862. The general import duties were brought down from 10 to $7\frac{1}{2}$ percent in 1864 and to 5 percent in 1875. Allthough these years import duties were imposed purely for revenue purposes without even a tinge of protective intention.[79]

Even so, about the year 1874, cotton duties, which contributed nearly half of the total revenue yielded by import duties, came under a severe attack from the Lancashire cotton manufacturers.[80] In 1874 the Manchester Chamber of Commerce addressed a memorial to the secretary of state complaining that a protected trade in cotton manufactures was growing up in India to the disadvantage both of India and Great Britain and asking for the abolition of the import duties on cotton manufactures. But committee appointed by the Government of India in Nov., 1874 rejected the contention that the duties were protective. The cause of free trade was, however, taken up most vigorously by the new conservative secretary ot state for India Lord Salisbury, who repeatedly impressed upon the Government of India the necessity of removing the import duties on cotton goods.[81] He stressed that their abolition was necessary on both economic and political grounds. First of all, he pointed out, protective duties were opposed to the general policy of free trade accepted by Great Britain. Secondly, they harmed the British producers by restricting the export of their manufacture to India. Thirdly, they were against the interests of the Indian people whose necessaries of life were made costlier by them. Lastly, they were not even in the true interests of the rising Indian textiles industry that was, because of them, growing upon unsound foundations under artificial stimulation. Furthermore, he remarked, the political reasons for early abolition of the cotton duties were equally imperative.[82] The prophetic insight revealed in his reasoning in this respect is reproduced from the original.

"The gradual transfer of the Indian trade from the english to the indian manufacturer, which appears likely to take place, will be attended with much bitterness of feeling on the one side, and with the keen anxiety for the security of an unexpected success upon the other. The english manufacturer will press with increasing earnestness for the abandonment of the duty to which he will imput his losses and in proportion to his urgency the indian manufacturer will learn to value it. Some soreness even now will be felt, and more will be expressed by persons who will trace such a policy to a preference of english over indian claims. But the irritation will only extend over a wider surface if action is delayed, and may, if the delay be too far prolonged, become a serious public danger."[83]

The whole controversy was conclusively settled, at least in so far as Lord Salisbury was concerned, in his despatch of 31 May, 1876. After re-examining the entire question, he declared that, the interests of India imperatively require the timely removal of a tax which is at once wrong in principle, injurious in its practical effect and self-destructive in its operations. The only remaining argument against the removal of the cotton duties was the harmful effect that it would have upon the exchequer ; and, in this respect, he laid down that, while the Government of India should use its discretion in implementing his directive, the abolition of these duties should have priority over every other form of fiscal relief to the Indian tax-payer.

The Government of India and the Viceroy, Lord Northbrook, were, however, not amenable to the prodding of the Secretary of State and refused to abandon the cotton duties on the ground that they were not in practice protective. But with a view of the critics, the government decided to impose 5 percent duty on the import of long-staple cotton.

The fact of the cotton import duties was, however sealed when the resignation of Lord Lytton as the Viceroy and of Sir John Strachey as the finance member, both of whom, were quite keen to comply with the wishes of the secretary of state.[84] At this time (on 11 July, 1877), the House of Commons passed a resolution to the effect that the duties now levied upon cotton manufactures imported into India, being protective in their nature, are contrary to sound commercial policy and ought to be repealed without delay as soon as the financial conditions of India will permit.[85] The enthusiasm of Lord Lytton and his finance minister was, however curbed to a certain extent by the financial stringency produced by the Afghan was, recurring famines and the depreciation of silver. Even so, the duties on certain coarser kinds of cotton goods were remitted in 1878 and in 1879 the duties on all cotton goods not containing yard of a count higher than 30 were remitted. Further opportunity came in 1882 when the budget showed a surplus of 3 millions. Cotton duties along with duties on most of the other commodities, were remitted in toto. Only the special duties on salt, wines and liquors, and arms and ammunition were allowed to remain.

For the next 12 years India was virtually without any tariff duties and conformed more nearly to the principles of free trade than any other country. Even the ports of Britain were less free than those of India. This naturally resulted in an increase in the import of manufactured goods, the value of these imports went up by 28 percent from 1878-79 to 1881-82 and 45% during 1878-79 to 1884-85. Since these were also the years of a steady fall in prices, the quantitative increase in India's imports was much greater. Admittedly, this increase was the product of many other factors and forces,. But, unquestionably, it was also in part due to the abolition of import duties.[86]

During the company's period, except Balasore where extensive salt trade was conducted, there was no other port built in the modern line. But after the abolition of salt monopoly the port of Balasore became desolate and deserted. It was only after the famine of 1866 the importance of developing ports was felt and the government spent huge sums to develop the ports like Balasore, Dhamrah, Chandabali, False-point, Ganjam and Gopalpur. It gave a fresh impetus to the export and import of commodities and invited the traders of Calcutta and import of commodities and invited the traders of Calcutta and England to establish trade in cotton piece and other consumer goods with Orissa through these ports. They in return sent forest produce, rice, oil seeds, coconuts from these ports. Thus the income from import and export duties began to increase during the second half of the 19th century.

The opening of railway line in 1890's accelerated the process of decline of ports as railway journey was safer and freight charges were also low. As a result the overseas trade and commerce of the province had dwindled and the income from the customs decreased.

(C) SYSTEM OF COLLECTION

Chowkeys or custom stations were established at different strategic places of Orissa for the collection of duties on the commodities of inland trade. Darogahs were incharge of these chowkeys. They were assisted by two constables and peons for the collection of duties. But for the collection of import and export duties on the commodities of overseas trade the custom houses or custom chowkeys were established in the different port towns of Orissa.

Each chowkey was managed by a Darogah or a Muharrier with the assistance of a few constables and peons. The salary of the Darogah varied from Rs. 12 to Rs. 20 per month. The salary of a Muharrier varied from Rs. 8 to Rs. 12 per month. The constables and peons were paid at the rate of Rs. 5 and Rs. 4 per month respectively. At the Sadar Office, there were a "Sherishtadar" and an english writer each with a salary of Rs. 40 per month besides a few Muharrier and peons. The total establishment of the government custom house at Balasore and several chowkeys stood at Rs. 366.3 annas per month on May 1, 1828.[87]

After the British occupation of Orissa, the government ordered the salt agent of Cuttack to take charge of the collection of customs of the province.[88] But the salt agent was busy in arranging and conducting the business of the salt department in which he faced considerable difficulties. He, therefore, reported to the Board of Trade on September 22, 1806, that he had no leisure to form any arrangement for the department of customs. He hoped to look into the matter in a subsequent period.[89] Truly speaking, the department of customs were properly organised only in 1810 when a new regulation was passed.

On April 10, 1810 the new regulations was passed for rescinding all regulations in force for collection of government customs in the provinces of Bengal, Bihar and Orissa and for re-establishing those duties with amended rules for their collections.[90] The custom house for the collection of government customs under this regulation was established in the town of Balasore for Orissa. It remained in charge of a collector of government customs, and he was subject to the authority of the Board of Revenue at the presidency. The regulation also enumerated the rates of duty to be levied on different articles and enlisted the articles which were to be exempted from the payment of such duties. It declared that the goods which paid the duty once should not be liable to the payment of any other duty. Of course, the 'rawanas' (certificate from the collector of customs) were to remain in force for one year only.

The collector of customs at Balasore kept proper vigilance on the proceedings of different chowkey officers. In case of complaints against them for fraudulent practices and illegal impositions prompt action was taken to enquire into the matter.[91]

When the office of the Commissioner of Revenue and circuit was created in 1829, it was provided that those officers throughout all divisions of the presidency should supervise and control several collectorships of customs within their respective jurisdictions. It was directed that in future the collectors of customs would correspond directly with the Commissioners of Revenue and circuit, and the orders of the commissioners, should be final in respect of all detentions, seizures, confiscations, remissions of fines or penalties and in the appointment of dismissal of uncovenanted officers. The Board of Customs, Salt and Opium was required to exercise a general power of control and supervision over the commissioners in such matters.[92]

A number of reasons can be ascribed to this poor collection of custom duties. Firstly, the number of vessels and its arrivals in the ports of their destination were not reported considerably. Many of the small craft that cleared out for Calcutta frequently disposed of their cargoes at Hijli and other such intermediate places between Balasore and Calcutta. Many of them remained in the neighbourhood of Calcutta and did not report themselves to the custom house.[93] Secondly, the amalas, darogahs and peons were indulged in corruptions. Thirdly, the smuggling of goods was rampant everywhere in Orissa. Fourthly, the government supervision was quite inadequate. Fifthly, the stall arrangement of the government was also unsatisfactory. W. White, the Master Attendant stated on July 29, 1857 that the services rendered to the several small ports of the district were insignificant. It only consisted in keeping of 2 peons in constant attendance to look after wrecked property and report the arrival and departures of vessels. There were neither buoyed nor beacons to point out the places and so the duties at those small ports were not levied properly.[94] Owing to all these reasons the collection of duties was unsatisfactory.

However, when the Act 22 of 1855 was passed for the regulation of ports and port dues by the Government of India, the collection began to increase. In 1858 a new act was passed (Act 11 of 1858) for the levy of port dues in certain ports in the province of Cuttack. Such ports were Balasore, Chudamani, Lochanpur, Channoah, Sartha, Subarnarekha and Dhamrah. In accordance with the new act, the ports dues were to be realised from May 1, 1858 at the rate of 6 annas for every one hundred maunds of burden in respect of every sea going vessel of the burden of 300 maunds and upwards which shall enter any of the said ports.[95]

But the collection of custom duties had gradually decreased after 1863. Firstly the abolition of salt monopoly in 1863 gave a death blow to the trade and commerce of the province. Secondly, the opening of railway lines after 1890's and the competition of railway companies which offered specially low rates for transport of goods led to the decline of Orissa's sea-borne trade and commerce. Only a few vessels had fortnightly services between the port of Gopalpur and Rangoon, Puri and Calcutta for passengers during the first half of the 20th century.[96]

In the matter of excise administration, the interest of the British government was materialised to a great extent. The unnoticeable and negligible excise revenue at the time of British conquest could be increased to the extent of Rs. 7,34,098 by the close of the century. The government not only legalised the process of manufacture of all excisable articles but also imposed new duties on various excisable articles affecting new administrative and legislative measures to fetch a significant excise revenue out of Orissa. The commercial activities of the people of Orissa was given a new lease of life by the establishment of a new regulated markets. By the beginning of the present century the government virtually monopolised the trade on all excisable articles. The aim of the Britisher at the time of conquest to Orissa could be successfully materialised through the monopolisation of the intoxicating, medicinal and excisable articles. The new zeal to monopolise the production of excisable articles and to collect more revenue as a perennial source of government revenue by selling these articles through incensed agents or vendors could be materialised. This new deal, however did not bring any substantial change on the economic life of the people of Orissa rather it was negation to the economic prosperity of the people.

Similarly, the British government adopted the same principle in the custom department to collect more revenue without much investment. The unplanned way of implementing new customs rates and customs rules allowed the Britishers only for more profit through portal trade evading the custom duties, with no gain for the Orissa traders. Several arrangements were made by the Britishers for high customs revenue but due to certain reasons portal trade declined. The silting of the rivers did not allow important ports to exists. The decline of portal trade and duties was caused as a volume of trade in the ports of Orissa were diverted towards the coast canal after it was being ready in 1887 to traffic. Merchants preferred inland trade as the cost of the portal trade was much higher due to the heavy pressure of custom duty. The extension of railways to Orissa contributed further in the decline of portal trade.

As trade was concerned the later part of the 19th century following the years of famine was marked by an impressive increase of portal trade by the government but on the other hand, there was no increase of wealth and comfort among the people of Orissa. It was because of the fact that the whole export trade was confined to food-grains and other raw products of nature and the import trade was confined to finished goods of Europe. However, the improvement of regular trade definitely gave this country an advantage of security against another famine with intensity. The expectation was that the development of ports and sea-borne traffic would effect a complete economic revolution for the government through the collection of customs revenue changing a backward, isolated and unimportant country into a busy and prosperous centre of trade did not prove true. Thus, the British policy of import and export depreciated the economy of the whole of Orissa.

REFERENCES

1. G. Toynbee, A sketch of the history of Orissa (1803-1828), Calcutta, 1873, p. 66.
2. Bengal judicial, consultations, 5 Sept., 1805, No. 26, Govt. of Bengal to Melville and Harcourt.
3. B. C. Ray, New lights an Maratha Orissa, Bhubaneswar, 1993, p. 213.
4. K. M. Patra, Orissa under the East India company, New Delhi, 1971, pp. 211-212.
5. G. Toynbee, op. cit, p. 66.
6. Bengal judicial (Civil) proceedings No. 27, 5 Sept. 1805, Commissioners of Orissa to Govt. of Bengal.
7. Proceedings of Board of Revenue (Misc.) No. 17, 29 Sept. 1819, Collector of Cuttack to Secretary to Board of Revenue.
8. Abstract of regulations of Government, Vol.IV, p. 119, Regulation No. 10, 1813.
9. G. Toynbee, A sketch of the history of Orissa (1803-1828), Calcutta, 1873, p. 66.
10. L.S.S.O.' Malley, Bengal District Gazetteers (Balasore), 1908, pp. 170-171.
11. Report on the administration of Excise, Revenue of lower provinces, 1911-12, p. 206.
12. L.S.S.O' Malley, op. cit, p. 171.
13. Report on the administration of Bengal, 1880-81, p. 49.
14. Report on the administration of Bengal, 1893-94, p. 66.
15. Report on the administration of Bengal, 1835-36, p. 98.
16. Report on the administration of Excise, Revenue of lower provinces, 1896-97, p.164.
17. Report on the administration of Excise, Revenue of lower provinces, 1905-06, p. 128.

18. Ibid, 1873, p.117.

19. Ibid, 1860-61, p. 71.

20. Ibid, 1873-74, p. 117.

21. Report on the administration of Excise, Revenue of lower provinces, 1872, p. 76.

22. Report on the administration of Bengal, 1880-81, p. 121.

23. Ibid, 1883-84, p.131.

24. Ibid, 1899-1900, p.245.

25. PBCSO, No. 22, May 21, 1846, Commissioner, Cuttack to Board of Customs, Salt and Opium, 18, 1846.

26. Cuttack Revenue Records, ACC. No. 93, Collector, Cuttack to Commissioner No. 120, August 13, 1830.

27. PBCSO, No. 44, April 20, 1838, Commissioner to take necessary action.

28. PBSCO, No. 31, April 29, 1847, Commissioner, Cuttack to Secretary, PBCSO, April 7, 1847.

29. General administration report of Orissa division, 1878-79, p. 31.

30. Bengal legislative council proceedings, Vol. XXX, 1898, February 26, 1898.

31. GAROD, 1899-1900, Pr. 105, p. 27.

32. Ibid, 1899-1900, Pr. 102, p. 27.

33. H. R. Ghosal, Economic transition in the Bengal presidency (1793-1833), p. 102.

34. Rundall's report, 1883, Para-14.

35. Report on the administration on Bengal, 1860-61, p. 23.

36. Rundall's report, 1883, Para-19.

37. Bengal revenue proceedings (Salt), April, 1863, Govt. of Madras to Govt. of India, No. 263, 6 February 1863.

38. Rundall's report, 1883, Para-19.

39. Salt report, 1874-75, Para-11.
40. Ibid.
41. Salt report, 1877-78, p. 2.
42. Salt report, 1878-79, p. 1.
43. Report on the administration of Bengal, 1881-82, Para-63.
44. Maddox report, Vol. 1, p. 421.
45. Early european travellers in the Nagpur territories, p. 4.
46. Ibid, p.52.
47. G. Toynbee, A sketch of the History of Orissa, (1803-1828), 1873, p. 88.
48. Bengal judicial (Civil) proceedings No. 26 of Sept. 5, 1805, Government several in Council to Commissioners at Cuttack, 1804.
49. Ibid.
50. Ibid.
51. Ibid.
52. Ibid.
53. H. T. Princep, History of political and military transactions in India, Vol. II, p. 432.
54. Bengal judicial (Civil) proceedings No. 7 of April 13, 1810, Regulation 9 of 1810, April 19, 1810.
55. Balasore customs house records (No. 586), Collector of Govt. of Customs to Secretary to Board of Customs, Salt and Opium, Aug, 1829.
56. Ibid, Collector of Govt. Customs to Civil Auditor, May, 21, 1828.
57. Board of revenue records (Custom Deptt. Vol No. 25A), Secretary to Govt. of Bengal to Commissioner at Cuttack, 7 July, 1820.
58. Ibid.
59. Balasore customs house records (Vol. No. 22), Collector of Govt. Customs to Commissioner at Cuttack, 20 July, 1824.

60. Board of Revenue Records, (Customs Dept. Vol. No. 25A), Accountant to Commissioner of Cuttack from 1816 to 1823 (*relevant portions).
61. Balasore customs house records (No. 586), Collector of Govt. customs to Secretary to Board of Customs, Salt and Opium, Aug. 13, 1829.
62. Ibid, No. 574, Collector of Govt. customs to Secretary to Board of Customs, Salt and Opium, May 17, 1825.
63. Ibid, Nov. 9, 1827.
64. Ibid.
65. Ibid, Collector of Govt. customs to Commissioner of Cuttack, August 13, 1829.
66. Ibid, Henry Rickets to Secretary to Board of Customs, Salt and Opium, Feb. 18, 1836.
67. Ibid, No. 91 of March 31, 1836, Statement of the collector of Govt. customs at Balasore, March 12, 1836.
68. Ibid, No. 90 of March 31, 1836, Henry Rickets to Secretary to Board of Customs, Salt and Opium, March 12, 1836.
69. Ibid, No. 92 of March 31, 1836, Board of Customs, Salt and Opium to Govt. of Bengal, March 31, 1836.
70. Balasore No. 92 of March 31, 1836, Board of Customs, Salt and Opium to Govt. of Bengal, March 31, 1836.
71. Proceedings of Board Revenue (Customs) No. 45 of March 27, 1855, Collector of Govt. customs to Secretary to Board of Revenue, March 8, 1851.
72. Ibid.
73. Balasore customs house records, No. 720, Collector of Salt, Customs to Henry Ricketts, Member, Board of Revenue, Nov. 25, 1853, No. 14.

74. Selection from records of Govt. Bengal, 1853, No. XXX, Report on the district of Balasore, Henry Rickets, 1853.
75. Balasore customs house records, No. 780, junior Secretary to Govt. of Bengal to Commissioner of Cuttack, May 8, 1857, No. 2117.
76. Ibid, White to collector of Balasore, June 1857, No. 95.
77. G.S. Fagon, Acts of the Legislative council of India, Vol. III, pp. 547-48.
78. Ibid.
79. Bipan Chandra, The Rise and Growth of Economic Nationalism in India, 1977, pp. 217-218.
80. The Imperial Gazetteers (1908), Vol. IV, p. 262.
81. The Secretary of States Despatch (Separate Revenue) No. 6, 15 July, 1815.
82. The Secretary of States Despatches (Legislative) of 11 Nov. 1815, No. 51.
83. Ibid, 15 July, 1875.
84. The History of Lord Lytton's Indian administration, 1876-1880 (London, 1899), pp.462.
85. Bipan Chandra, Op. Cit, pp. 220-221.
86. J. Stratchey, India (London 1903), pp. 181-182.
87. Balasore Custom House Records (ACC No. 586), Collector of Govt. Customs to Civil Auditor, May 21, 1828.
88. Proceedings of Board of Ṭrade (Customs), Govt. of Board of Trade, Dec. 5, 1805, Vol. 20, pp. 684-685.
89. Ibid, Collector of customs to Board of Trade, Sept. 22, 1806, Vol 23, p. 220.
90. Bengal judicial (civil) proceedings, No.7, of April 3, 1810 (Regulation 9 of 1810, April 10, 1810).
91. Proceedings of Board of Revenue (Cutsoms) No. 15, of Nov. 16, 1813, Collector of Govt. Customs

to Secretary to Board of Revenue, Oct., 27, 1813.

92. Proceedings of Board of Customs, Salt and Opium, No. 28 of April 3, 1829, Orider of the Vice-president in Council, Feb., 26, 1829.
93. Proceedings of the Board of Revenue (Customs) No. 44 of March 27, 1851, Collector of Govt. Customs to Secretary to Board of Revenue, March 8, 1851.
94. Balasore Customs House Records Act No. 780, White to Collector of Balasore, July 29, 1857.
95. G.S. Fagan, Acts of the Legislative Council of India, Vol. III, pp. 574-548.
96. Madras district gazetteers, Ganjam district, Vol. II, Madras, 1930, pp. 166-167.

Chapter - 7

CONCLUSION

The nineteenth century witnessed certain economic forces at work in Europe which had its far-reaching impact on India as well as Orissa. The industrial revolution, which championed the growth of free-trade theory, broke out during the later part of the 18th century. It made England extremely zealous to acquire new territories for economic exploitation and political domination. This necessitated the Britishers to take possession of new territories. Orissa was one of them and they conquered it in 1803 defeating the Marathas. The interest of the East India company to take possession of the province of Orissa was to complete the kind of communication between the province of Orissa was to complete the kind of communication between the territories under the Bengal and Madras governments for commercial and strategic necessity. The change of government from Marathas to Britishers brought about significant changes in the field of communication, industry, trade, commerce and the economic life of the people of Orissa. Thus, the nineteenth century was a period of transition in the history of Orissa in the field of economic development.

The East India company ruled Orissa from 1803 to 1857. It accelerated the process of economic decline of Orissa. During the company's rule, Orissa seemed to have been left singularly neglected and thereby denied of many advantages. The officers and servants of the company adopted an attitude of aversion to the Oriyas. Unfortunately, the company looked upon Orissa either as an administrative appendage of Bengal or just a territorial link between Bengal and Madras. British government introduced radical changes in the field of currency and trade. In 1805, they introduced salt monopoly which caused slow rise of prices of essential commodities. In 1811, the government abolished the age old cowry currency which exterted an adverse effect on the economy. The reaction of the people to this and other ecomomic exploitations took the shape of resistance movement in Khurda under the leadership of Buxi Jagabandhu Vidhyadhar in 1817.

Introduction of salt monopoly, policy of laissez-faire, abandonment of policy of investment, importation of Liverpool salt and machine made textile goods paved the way for the economic decline of Orissa. The East India company had concentrated all attention on maximum returns as profit. Dividends first and last, was the slogan of the government under the company. While the company carried away 38 lakhs of rupees per year and an average by way of taxes, the development of means of communication, education, irrigation, industries were almost neglected. Orissa at the end of the company's rule remained lamentably backward in every field. The consequences of such an apathy could not be realised by the servants of the company during their administration.

Thus, an ominous future was stored for Orissa. Within 8 years of the end of the company's rule in 1866, Orissa fell a victim to the famine of most intense and desolating character which took away one-third of her entire population. The Orissa famine was like an epitaph in the East India company's rule. The first phase of the British rule in Orissa is rightly characterised as the period of stagnation and economic deterioration.

The great famine of 1866 was a watershed and an eye-opener in the history of Orissa. The famine which claimed the life of one-third population of Cuttack, Puri and Balasore three densely populated districts of Orissa, exposed the hollowness of British claim of benign rule. After the searching inquiry into the cause of mortality of about one million people, the British administrators gave up their attitude of complacency. The famine commission presided over by Sir George Campbell made several recommendations for the prevention of famine in future. With this object in view, they started taking more interest than before for the economic development of Orissa specially in the field of communication, trade, import, export and industry.

Communication, an important infra-structure of the economic development of a state was less understood in Orissa during the first half of the 19th century under the British rule. That's why economy of Orissa remained underdeveloped for a fairly long period. Orissa had no good system of communication before famine. Roadways and waterways were generally unmetalled, not properly bridged and impassable during rains. Communication was confined to improving cart tracks, not a single all weather road existed, port facilities were either not fully developed or waning out. The means of communication was in backward condition causing enormous inconvenience to the people and insurmountable obstacles to the social, political and economic growth of the state. The famine commission recommended for speedy improvement in roads, canals and ports to provide transport to different parts of Orissa to break isolation. Though permanent improvement of the ports of Orissa was not undertaken, yet the ports of Orissa were improved after the famine. Cuttack was connected with false-point. The coast canal was opened in 1887 connecting Hooghly at Goenkhali with the river Matai at Charbatia. Other navigable canals connected various places of Orissa with ports and with Calcutta. The grand trunk road, the most important highway connected Calcutta and Madras. A real revolution in the field of communication came with the opening of the Bengal-Nagpur railways during the closing years of 19th century. The railways placed Calcutta within a few hours reach of Balasore, Cuttack and Puri. Thus, it can be said without a shadow of doubt that there was the improvements of communication in Orissa after 1866, but these were too inadequate to cater to the needs of the people.

There was brisk trade after the great famine of Orissa in 1866 with the development of communication. It increased in value with the passing of years. It is true that it showed a familiar colonial pattern. The British-Indian government controlled trade and industry purely with a view to foster British interests. Orissa no doubt underwent a commercial revolution which integrated it with the world market but she was forced to occupy a subordinate position. Foreign trade took big strides forward especially after 1858 increasing from Rs. 15 crores in 1834 to Rs. 60 crores in 1858 and Rs. 213 crores in 1899. But this growth did not represent a positive feature in Orissan economy nor did it contribute to the welfare of the people of Orissa. Incorporation of foreign goods led to the destruction of local industries and trade. The increase in import trade was certainly an indication of improvement but there was no increased wealth and comfort of people of Orissa. The growth of the Orissan trade was neither natural nor normal ; it was artificially fostered to serve British imperialism.

Overseas trade of Orissa was designed to serve the interests of British imperialism during the period under review. It adversely affected the economy of Orissa. It proved to be more harmful, than helpful. The worst feature of maritime trade of British Orissa was that outside vessels had displaced Orissa's sea-going vessels and outside merchants had captured her trade. In course of time, markets of Orissa were flooded with machinemade goods which were obviously of superior in quality and sold at a cheaper rate. The collapse of rural artisan industries was caused largely by competition with the cheaper imported machinemade goods from England. It contributed to the improverishment of peasants and artisan classes. The cotton weaving and spinning and salt industries were the worst hit. The influx of foreign goods and consequent destruction of Orissa's weaving and salt industries, continuous export of rice from Orissa and consequent scarcity of foodgrains and handling of maritime trade by outside merchants proved most harmful.

The deterioration of ports, opening of coast canal and the advent of railways affected adversely the overseas trade of the province. Trade was brisk, but since it consisted only in port of foodgrains and import of manufactures, the material prosperity of the province did not increase in the same proportion as the increase in the volume of trade.

Orissa had a long established reputation in many cottage industries from time immemorial especially weaving, salt and metal work. The filigree industry had attracted the attention of Europeans from medieval time. But during 19th century, it was unfortunate that these traditions crippled due to the British policy. Orissa was not industrialised during this period. The direct cause was lack of interest on the part of those who had capital with them. They were mostly people who came as land holders from Bengal and they diverted the surplus capital from Orissa to Calcutta market. It was but obvious that at the cost of suffering of Orissa, a belt of industries developed on the banks of the river Hooghly. A large number of families lost their livelihood due to the closure of cottage industries and due to the importation of British made cloths. When one economic group in the society was disturbed the other economic groups in the society like carpenters, potters, agricultural labourers and farmers were bound to suffer. The ruin of the indigenous industries and the absence of other avenues of employment forced millions of craftsmen to crowd into agriculture. The pressure of population on land increased. Thus, the impact of British traders on cottage industries was both restrictive and harmful. The people of the province could not receive the good results of the industrial revolution which began during this period.

Salt was an established and prosperous indigenous industry of Orissa which produced the finest salt of India. As an established industry, Orissa used to export more than three lakhs of mounds of salt annually during the closing years of the previous Maratha rule. The British administration controlled it through monopoly and after the abolition of monopoly, in 1863, through excise system and finally they closed the whole sea-coast of Orissa from the manufacture of salt. Finally, the salt industry in Orissa perished. Along with it ended the only means of circulation of money and a favourable trade. The diversity of occupations which it also provided was lost. The policy of direct state assistance to industry was not in conformity with laissez-faire philosophy of English economist. The consequences of the British salt policy in Orissa was disastrous from many directions. Firstly, the price of salt increased which caused hardship to the people. Secondly, with the abolition of monopoly the manufacture of the articles declined and many poor salt workers were thrown into unemployment. The importation of cheap Liverpool salt finally resulted the closure of this profitable Orissa industry. Being thrown out of their traditional profession, the salt workers joined the class of agricultural labourers. Some of them left their native places to distant places of Assam and Burma for their livelihood. Thus, the destruction of salt trade produced ruinous effect on the economy of the province and the general welfare of the people which also retarded the prosperity of the province.

Import and export duties formed an important aspect in the field of trade. The British government after the conquest of Orissa expressed their keen interest on import and export duties and decided to make it as an important source of revenue collection. The Britishers not only realised the process of manufacture of all excisable articles but also imposed new duties on various excisable articles to fetch a significant excise revenue out of Orissa. The commercial activities of the people of Orissa was given a new lease of life by the establishment of new regulated markets. The aim of the Britishers to monopolies the production of excisable articles and to collect more revenue as a perennial source of government revenue was materialised. The unnoticeable and negligible excises revenue at the time of British conquest could be increased to the extent of Rs. 7,34,098/- by the close of the 19th century, but they spent nothing for the welfare of the people. The increase of consumption of these articles and the implementation of new excise rules in different times enabled the government to yield more revenue, but there was no substantial change on the economic life of the people of Orissa; rather it had an adverse effect on the economic prosperity of the people.

The callousness and disinterestedness of the British officials were the potent factors for the economic backwardness of the people of Orissa. Orissa could not receive the proper attention of the British officers. Most of them were unable to understand the economic problems. Much of Orissa remained in deep and inaccessible forests. The British officers had to depend on the subordinate officers' opinion and suggestion.

This was one of the reasons why many of the problems concerned with trade, industry and communication could not be examined by the competent officers. This was not the case in other provinces. Therefore, Orissa's economy had little chance to emancipate where as the other provinces were ahead on the road of economic prosperity and industrial growth.

Despite the above adverse effects of British trade policy in Orissa of 19th century, it had certain advantages. There were some improvements of communications. Some roads were metalled. Bridges were constructed and railway lines opened to traffic. The development of roads, railways, navigable canals and ports not only broke Orissa's isolation from the outside world but also facilitated export and import trade by providing mobility to the people to move to different places in search of employment and reduced the liability of the province of famines. As a result, the socio-economic and cultural link of Orissa with other parts of India began. The development of communication encouraged more people to visit Lord Jagannath. The geographical isolation of Orissa came to an end. Trade received impetus with the introduction of modernised and uniform system of coinage, weights and measures. Tax system was simplified and modernised export and import trade increased. The establishment of markets in central places facilitated internal trade but profits went to the outsiders as very small number of Oriyas participated in trade. On the whole, it can be said that the foundation of a new economic system of Orissa was laid during this period under review, but to be beneficial to the interests of imperialistic ruler but not to that of the ruled.

Considered from different angles of view it may be said in conclusion that the British trade policy in Orissa (1803-1900) left a legacy of stagnation, unpredictable economic deterioration before the outbreak of famine which was accentuated by a process of stabilisation and a comparative prosperity following the years of famine. The continuous drain upon the provincial economy with no equivalent return of any kind led to the accumulating poverty of the people that accounts for the economic backwardness of the province throughout the 19th century. But British historians, however, failed to notice the exploitative nature of the British rule, put undue emphasis on the beneficial character of the Raj an blamed natural hindrances like floods, low productivity of the soil as impediments to industrial development. Thus, Orissa was closely tied in matters of trade policy to the British interests than to the true interests of the people of Orissa.

BIBLIOGRAPHY

(Consulted at the National Archieves of India, New Delhi ; National Library, Calcutta ; Orissa State Archieves, Bhubaneswar ; West Bengal State Archieves, Calcutta and Board of Revenue Library, Cuttack).

PRIMARY SOURCES

A. Manuscripts-Official Records (Unpublished and correspondences)

Bengal Revenue Proceedings from 1815-1900

500 volumes have been consulted containing

(i)Bengal Revenue Proceedings - Land Revenue.

(ii)Bengal Revenue Proceedings-Miscellaneous.

(iii)Bengal Revenue Proceedings-Customs.

(iv)Bengal Revenue Proceedings-Salt.

(v)Bengal Revenue Proceedings-Finance, Separate Revenue, Salt.

(vi)Bengal Revenue Proceedings-Excise.

Proceedings of Board of Customs, Salt and Opium, 1819-1890, 50 volumes.

Proceedings of Bengal Legislative Council, 1850-1889, 30 volumes

Proceedings of the Board of Revenue, Miscellaneous, Customs and Excise, 1805-1890, 40 volumes.

Proceedings of Bengal Public Works Department,

1862, 1863, 1868 and 1869, 4 volumes.

Balasore Salt Records, 1803-1875, 65 volumes.

Balasore Custom House Records, 1805-1875, 25 volumes.

Board's Revenue Collections, Vol. 582-587, 6 volumes.

Bengal Revenue Consultations, 1822.

Cuttack Revenue Records, 1803-1820, 17 volumes.

Cuttack Salt Records, 1803-1875, 70 volumes.

Records of the Board of Revenue, Lower province, File No. 125, File No. 66 of 1892.

Records of the Board of Revenue,

File No. 93, of 1878 (Excise)

File No. 91 of 1891 (Excise)

File No. 159 of 1894 (Customs)

File No. 35 of Collection of Government Customs, Records of the Customs Department, 1820-1827, 5 volumes. Salt and Excise Records.

Letter No. 665S, 1901, Assistant Commissioner, 24 Parganas to Commissioner, Excise, Bengal.

Letter No. 46, 1901, Commissioner, Excise, Salt, Bengal to Secretary, Government of India.

Letter No. 655TF, 1901, Secretary, Government of Bengal to Secretary, Government of India.

Copy of a letter, September, 1, 1806, R. Ker, Magistrate, Cuttack to Board of Revenue.

Public Works Department, Govt. of India civil works.

(a) Communication, 1860-1885.

(b) Railways, 1879-1885.

(c) Miscellaneous, 1860-1885.

Selection from records of the Bengal Government, No. XXXV (Reports of the districts of Puri and Balasore, Henry Ricket, 1853), Calcutta, 1859.

Selection from records of the Bengal Government, XXIV, No. 3 (Papers on the settlement of Cuttack and on the state of Tributary mahals,) Calcutta, 1867.

Selection of records on Feudatory states of Orissa divisions and rules applicable to them, Part I, Calcutta, 1907 (Confidential).

Printed Sources (Records)

A selections from a government records and documents, A collection of treaties, engagements and sunnads relating to India and neighbouring countries, C. V. Aitchison (Ed.) Volume I to V, Calcutta, 1862-1864.

A hand book of the Bihar and Orissa provincial records 1771 to 1859, Patna, 1933.

Bengal manuscript records, A selected list of 14136 letters in the Board of Revenue, Calcutta, 1782-1807 in 4 volumes (Ed.), W. W. Hunter, London, 1894.

Guide to Orissa records, Volumes 1 to III, S. C. De (Ed.), Orissa State Archieves, Bhubaneswar, 1961-62.

B. Reports

Abstract of regulation of government, W. Blunt (Compiler), 1826-28, 4 volumes.

Administration of Bengal under Sir Andrew Fraser (1903-1908), Calcutta, 1908.

Acts of Legislative Council of India, Fagan (Ed.),

Vol.II, Calcutta, 1862.

An Industrial Survey of Orissa, H. B. Mohanty, Cuttack, 1952.

A few notes on cotton and cotton stuff in the district of Cuttack, Calcutta, 1897.

Annual report of the Director of Industries, Govt. of Bihar and Orissa (year-wise), 1920-21, 1924-25.

A rough survey of the cottage industries in Orissa, Rai Bahadur B. C. Pattanaik.

A monography on the silk fabrics of Bengal, W. G. Mukherjee, Calcutta, 1903.

Annual report of the Director of Industries, Orissa.

Bihar and Orissa, First decennial review (1912-22) of the administration and development of the province, Patna, 1923.

Calender of persian correspondence, 4 volumes, Records department, Calcutta, 1911-1949.

Diary of Streynsham Master, T. Richard (Ed.), Vol.II, London, 1911.

Diary of Willium Hedges, Colonel Henry (Ed.), London, LXXXVIII.

Early European travellers in Nagpur territories, Nagpur, 1930.

East India report of Famine Commission presented to both Houses of the Parliament, London, 1881.

Final report on the survey and settlement of the province of Orissa, S. L. Maddox, 1890-1900, Vol. I and II, Calcutta, 1900.

Final report on the revision settlement of Orissa, J. F. W. James, 1906-1912.

Final report on the survey and settlement of Khurda government estate, Taylor and Maddox, 1897-1898, Calcutta, 1901.

Final report on the survey and settlement of Balasore district, D. H. Kingsford, Calcutta, 1900.

Final report on the Survey and Settlement of Puri district, H. Mcpherson, Calcutta, 1900.

Final report of the select committee of the House of Commons in the affairs of East India Company, 1812.

General administration report of Orissa division (Annual), 1850 to 51 to 1898-99, 49 volumes.

History of Portuguese in Bengal.

Memoirs of the map of Mughal empire, J. Runnel PC XXX, London, 1793.

Memoirs of the Bengal Civilian, J. Beams, London, 1861.

Memorandum of the revenue administration of Bengal, D. E. Mcneil, Calcutta, 1873,

Memorandum on the results of Indian administration during the past 50 years of British rule, Calcutta, 1908.

Moral and material progress report (Annual volumes) from 1864-65 to 1904-05, 1911-12.

Narrative of the Principal Events, H. P. Prinsep (Ed.) 1813-14, London, 1820.

Narrative of the Principal Events connected with Flood embarkment in Orissa and the origin and development of Orissa canals, 1840-1900, W. A. English, Calcutta, 1900.

Proceedings of Bihar and Orissa Legislative Council, 1919.

Quinquennial administration report, Orissa division, 1900-1901 to 1904-1905.

Report on the administration of Bengal (Annual) 1830-1831 to 1880-1881, 50 volumes.

Report on the rise of prices and wages (1914), 3 volumes with statistical appendices, K. L. Datta.

Report on the administration of Salt department, 1830-1831, to 1885-1886, 55 volumes.

Report on the administration of Salt revenue in Madras Presidency and Orissa, 1866, 1867, 2 volumes.

Report on the Abkari revenue of Lower province, 1845-1846, Calcutta 1847.

Report on the Abkari revenue of Lower province, 1852-1853, Calcutta, 1854.

Report on the Abkari revenue of Lower province, 1857-1858, Calcutta, 1859.

Report on the Abkari revenue of Lower province. 1862-1863, Calcutta, 1864.

Report on the Abkari revenue of Lower province, 1880-1881, Calcutta, 1882.

Report on the Salt in British India, Bengal, Part II & III, Volume 25 & 26, George Plowden.

Report of the Commissioners appointed to enquire into the Famine of Bengal and Orissa, 1866, 2 volumes.

Report of Orissa Famine Commission, 1866 with Appendix.

Report of the Indian Famine Commission, 1880, Part I.

Report of the Indian Famine Commission, 1898 with evidence volume.

Report of the Commissioners appointed to enquire into certain matter in connection with the Orissa canals, 1884-1885.

Report on the Mahanadi river, 1881, A. Cotton, Calcutta.

Report on the river Mahanadi and its distributaries, 1863, R. Temple.

Report on the district of Balasore, Henry Ricket, Calcutta, 1858.

Report on the Bay of Bengal, False-point and Jumboo Port, Patna, 1923. Cartright Reid.

Report on the manufacture of salt and the system of administration of Salt revenue of Balasore, Cuttack, and Puri districts forming the Orissa division of Bengal presidency, 1883, C. Rundall.

Report on the Indian Hemp and Drug commission, 1893-94.

Report on the administration of Feudatory states of Orissa, 1908-1909.

Report on the maritime trade of Bihar and Orissa (1935-36), Patna, 1937.

Report on the district of Midnapur and Cuttack, Calcutta, 1858.

Report on the administration of Customs department, Bengal presidency, 1874-75.

Report on the possibility of establishment of Salt Industry in coastal areas of Orissa. 1938, Indian Annual Register, Vol.I.

Report on the administration of excise revenue of Lower Provinces 1911-12.

C. Travel accounts and diaries

A voyage to Bengal or news from the East Indies, William Bruton, Vol. VIII, 1752.

A geographical account of countries round the Bay of Bengal, 1669 to 1679, Thomas Bowery, Ed. by Richard Temple, London, 1905.

A new account of the East Indies being observations and remarks of Capt. Alexander Hamilton, 2 vols. London, 1930.

D. Gazetteers

Imperial Gazetteers of India, 16 vols., 1881-1887 (relevant vols).

Bengal District Gazetteers (Cuttack) Calcutta, 1906.

Bengal District Gazetteers (Balasore) Calcutta, 1907.

Bengal District Gazetteers-Puri (Calcutta, 1907)

Bengal District Gazetteers-Sambalpur (Calcutta, 1908)

Bengal District Gazetteers-Angul (Calcutta, 1908.)

Cobden Ramsay, L.E.B., Bengal District Gazetteers-Feudatory States of Orissa, Calcutta, 1919.

Bihar and Orissa Gazetteer, Cuttack, Puri and Balasore, L.S.O. Malley, Calcutta, 1929.

Orissa District Gazetteers-Koraput (Cuttack, 1945).

Orissa District Gazetteers-Koraput (Cuttack, 1966).

Orissa District Gazetteers-Cuttack (Cuttack, 1996).

Orissa District Gazetteers-Puri (Cuttack, 1977).

Orissa District Gazetteers-Balasore (Cuttack, 1992).

Orissa District Gazetteers-Sambalpur (Cuttack).

Orissa District Gazetteers-Ganjam (Cuttack, 1995).

Orissa District Gazetteers-Dhenkanal (Cuttack, 1972).

The Ganjam District Manual (Madras, 1918)

Manual of the District Vizagpatam (Madras, 1869)

Statistical account of Bengal, Vol. XIX, District of Puri and Orissa Tributary States, (London, 1877).

Puri District Gazetteers, Statistics, 1900-1901, to 1910-11 (Patna, 1915).

E. Contemporary Newspapers and Periodicals

English :

Bengal Past and Present

Bharati-Utkal university journal, Humanities, Vol. VIII, July, 1874, No. 14, Calcutta, Review.

Indian Antiquary.

Indian Economic and Social History Review.

Indian Historical Quarterly.

Journal of Asiatic Society of Bengal.

Journals of Bihar and Orissa Research Society.

Journals of Kalinga Historical Research Society.

Journals of Royal Asiatic Society of Bengal.

Orissa Historical Research Journal (several volumes)

Proceedings of Indian History Congress.

Proceedings of Orissa History Congress.

The Hindu Patriot

The Englishman

The Friends of India

The Economic and Political weekly, Vol.IX, No. 44, Nov. 2, 1874.

The Orissa past and present (Ed.) P. Parija, Utkal university.

The Statesman.

Young India, 1920-21.

Oriya :

Utkal Dipika, 1866-1905.

Utkal Putra, 1873.

Utkal Hitaisini, 1874.

The Sambalpur Hitaisini, 1869-1901.

The Balasore Sambad Bahika, 1870-1872.

Asha (Oriya daily)

The Samaj (Oriya daily)

Utkal Prasanga

SECONDARY SOURCES

BOOKS (ENGLISH)

Acharya, P., : Studies in Orissan History, Archaeology and Archieves (Baripada, 1969).

Agarwal, S. C. : The Salt Industry in India, Simla, 1937.

Ahmed, Z. A. : Some aspects of Economic and Financial aspects of British rule in India, Allahabad, 1937.

Ambhirajan. S, : Classical, Political economy and British policy in India, New Delhi, 1978.

Banerjee, R. D. : History of Orissa, 2 Vol, Calcutta, 1930-31.

Banerjee, P. N. : History of Indian Taxation, London, 1930 and Indian finance in the days of the company, London, 1928.

Basham, A. L. : The Wonder that was India, London, 1954.

Basu, B. D. : Ruin of Indian Trade and Industries,

Calcutta, 1935.

Beams, J.: Memories of a Bengal civilian, London, 1961.

Belgrum, Sayed Aulad Haidar : History of Subah-Bihar and Orissa in the 19th Century (Urdu), Calcutta,1915.

Bhatia, B. M. : Famines in India, London, 1967.

Bhattacharya, V. R. : New Face of Rural India, New Delhi, 1984.

Bhattacharya, S. : Financial foundations of the British Raj, Simla, 1920.

Bhola, S. C. : British economic policy in Orissa, New Delhi,1990.

Bose, C. N. : Thoughts on the economic condition of Bengal, its present and probable future, Calcutta, 1869.

Buckland, C. E. : Bengal under Lieutenant Governors, Vol. I, 1902.

Capper, John : Three Presidencies of India, London, 1853.

Cambridge History of India, Vol.VI, Revised edition, Delhi, 1958.

Campbell, George : Memoirs of my Indian Career, 2 Vols. London, 1895.

Chandra, Bipin : The rise and growth of economic nationalism in India, 1900-1905, Delhi 1977 ; Nationalism and colonialism in modern India, New Delhi, 1979.

Chesney, G. C. : Indian polity, London, 1868.

Choudhury, Benoy : Growth of commercial agriculture in Bengal 1757-1900, Vol.I, Calcutta, 1964.

Choudhury, S. N. : Economic history of colonialism,

Delhi, 1979.

Coupland, Sir Reginald : The Indian problems 1833-1835, Reprint, Bombay, 1969.

Cobden, Ramsay, L.E.B. : Feudatory States of Orissa, Calcutta, 1984 (Reprint).

Cunninghan, H. S. : British India and its rulers, London, 1881.

Das, Binod Sankar : Studies in economic history of Orissa from ancient times to 1833, Calcutta, 1978.

Das, P. C. : The Economic history of Orissa in the 19th century, New Delhi, 1989.

Dash, Sriram Chandra and Pandit Gopabandhu : Gopabandhu Sahitya Mandira, Cuttack, 1966.

Das, M. N. : Economic and Social development of modern India, Calcutta,1959. (Ed.) Sidelights on history and culture of Orissa (Cuttack, 1977)

Dantwala, M. I. : Poverty in India then and now, 1870-1970, Bombay 1973.

Desai, A. R. : Social background of Indian nationalism, Bombay, 1966.

Desai, T. B. : Economic history of India under British, Bombay,1968.

Dharma, Kumar (Ed.) : The Cambridge economic history of India, Vol.II, Delhi, 1984.

Digby, W. : Prosperous British India, London, 1891.

Dodwell, H. H. (Ed.) : The Cambridge history of India, Vol V, Delhi, 1968.

Dutta, K. K. : Alivardi and his Times, Calcutta, 1939, Survey of India's social life and economic condition in the 18th century

(1707-1813) ,Calcutta, 1961.

Dutta R. C. : The Economic history of India, 2 Vols, Government of India publications, Delhi, 1976. Famines in India, London, 1900.

Dutt, R. P. : India Today, Second revised edition, Bombay, 1949.

Fitchett, W. H. : The Tale of the Great Mutiny, London, 1911.

Fraser, Lovat : India under Curzon and After, London, 1911.

Fraser, Sir Andrew : Among Indian Rajas and Ryots, London, 1911.

Frazer, R. W. : British India, 1st. edn., London, 1896.

Gadgil, D. R. : Industrial evolution of India, Calcutta, 1924.

Gandhi, Mahatma : Satyagraha, Navajivan Prakashana, Ahmedabad, 1951.

Ganguli, B. N. : Reconstruction of India's Foreign Trade, Calcutta, 1946.

Garrat, G. T. : Rise and fulfillment of British rule in India, London, 1934.

Ghosal, H. R. : The Economic transition in the Bengal presidency, Calcutta, 1966.

Gopal, S. British policy in India, 1858-1905, Cambridge, 1965. The vice royalty of Lord Rippon, 1881-84, London, 1965.

Gopal, Lallaji, : The Economic life of north Indian, Delhi, 1965.

Griffith, Sir Percival : The British impact of India, London, 1952.

Haquė, M. A. : Muslim-administration in Orissa,

Calcutta, 1980.

Hamilton W. A. : A geographical, statistical and historical description of hindustan and the adjacent countries, 2 Vols., London, 1872.

Hunter, W. W. : History of Orissa, 2 Vols., London, 1872.

-The Annals of rural Bengal, Calcutta, 1965.

-Statistical account of Bengal, Vol. XIX, London, 1877.

Jit, N. K. : The Agrarian life and the economy of Orissa, 1833-1897, Calcutta, 1984.

Jena, K. C. : The Ascendancy of the British Raj in Orissa, Calcutta, 1982. Socio-economic conditions of Orissa during nineteenth century, Delhi, 1978.

Kaye, J. W. : The administration of the East India Company, London, 1859.

Kaushal, G. : Economic history of India, 1757-1966, New Delhi, 1979.

Kulkarni, V. B. : British statesmen in India, Orient Longmans, 1961.

Laurie, F. B. : Orissa, The garden of Superstition and Idolatry, London, 1820, p. 131.

Long Andrew : Life and letters of Sir Stafford Northcote, 2 Vols, London, 1890.

Loveday : A history and economics of Famines in India, London, 1914.

Lyall, A. : The rise and expansion of British dominion in India, London, 1920.

Mahtab, H. K.: History of Orissa, 2 Vols, Cuttack 1959 and 1960.

-(Ed.) History of Freedom movement in Orissa Vol. I-V, Cuttack, 1959.

Majumdar, R. C. : History and culture of Indian people, Bombay, 1963, Vol. IX.

Marx : Capital (Moscow edition), Vol.I to III (Articles on India), People's Publicity House.

Marshman, J. C : The History of India, Vol.II, London, 1867.

Masani, R. P. : Britain in India, Bombay, 1962.

Matcalf, Thomas : The Aftermath of revolt in India, Priceton, 1964.

Menon, V. P. : The transfer of power in India, Calcutta, 1957.

Mill, James : The History of British India, Vol.I, III, Reprint, New Delhi, 1972.

Mishra, B. K : Famines and poverty in India, New Delhi, 1991.

Mishra, Krupasindhu : Utkal Itihasa, Cuttack, 1933.

Mishra, Probodha Kumar : The political history of Orissa, Delhi, 1979.

Mishra, Sadasiva : Economic Survey of Orissa, 2 Vols, Govt. of Orissa, Bhubaneswar, 1960.

Mohanty, Balaram : Introducing Orissa, Bhubaneswar, 1979.

Mohanty, Nivedita : Oriya Nationalism, New Delhi, 1982.

Mohapatra, J. N. : Orissa in 1936-37 and 1938-39, Cuttack, 1941.

Mohapatra, R. R. : Some aspects of the economic Life of Orissa (C. 1550-1751), Bhubaneswar, 1984.

Muir, Ramsay : The Making of British India, Manchester, 1915.

Mukherjee, P. : History of Orissa, Vol. VI, Utkal University, 1904.

Mukherjee, Radha Kamal. : The Economic history of India, Allahabad 1967.

Munshi, K. M. : End of an Era, Bombay, 1957.

Narain, Brij : Indian Economic Life, Past and Present, Lahore, 1929.

Naroji, Dedabhai : Poverty and un-British rule in India, London, 1901.

O. Malley, L.S.S. : History of Bengal, Bihar and Orissa under British rule, Calcutta, 1925. Modern India and West London, 1968.

Oswen, G. D. : Sketches of Rules, 3 Vols., Oxford, 1908.

Oxford History of India, Oxford, 1958.

Pal, Dharma : Administration of Sir John Lawrence, 1864-1869, Simla, 1952.

Panikar, K. M. : A Survey of Indian History, Bombay, 1966.

Pattanaik, G. C. : The Famine and some aspects of the British economic policy in Orissa, 1866-1905, Cuttack,1980.

Pattanaik, J. : Feudatory states of Orissa, Vol. II (Allahabad, 1988), p. 525.

Pattanaik, P. K. : A forgotten chapter of Orissan history, Calcutta, 1979.

Patra, K. M. : Orissa under East India Company, New Delhi, 1971.

Philips, C. H. : The East India Company, 1784-1834, Oxford, 1961.

Prasad, Amba : Indian Railway-A study in public

utility administration, London, 1960.

Rai, Lajpat : England's Debt to India, New York, 1917.

Ranade, M. G. : Essays on Indian Economic, London, 1906.

Ray, B. C. : Foundation of British Orissa, Cuttack, 1960.

Orissa under the Marathas, 1751-1803, Allahabad, 1960

Orissa under the Mughals, Calcutta, 1981.

New lights on Maratha Orissa, Bhubaneswar, 1993.

Rath, Radhanath : The story of freedom movements in Orissa, Cuttack, 1964.

Robert, P. E. : History of British India under the company and the crown, Oxford, 1938.

Roberts, Lord : Forty-one years in India, 2 Vols. London, 1897.

Roy, S.C. : The Hill Bhuyan of Orissa, Ranchi, 1935.

Rusden, R. D, : The Indian salt tax, Speech at the Annual meeting of the Manchester Chambers of Commerce, Feb 9, 1881.

Sahu N. K., (Ed.) : A History of Orissa, Vol. II, Calcutta, 1950. New aspects of the History of Orissa, Sambalpur, 1971.

Sahu, Bhagaban : Princely states of Orissa under the British crown (1858-1905), Cuttack, 1993.

Samal, J. K. : Orissa under the British crown, 1858-1905, New Delhi, 1973.

Sarkar, Sir Jadunath : India through ages, Calcutta, 1950.

-Economic history of India, Calcutta, 1917.

Sarkar, B. K. : Transport and communication in India, 1925.

Sen, Amartya : Poverty and Famine, Oxford, 1981.

Sen, S. N. : Eighteen Fifty Seven, New Delhi, 1957.

Sen, S. P. and Ray, N. R. : Modern Bengal : a socio-economic survey, Calcutta, 1973.

Sitaramayya, Pattabhi : History of Indian National Congress, Bombay, 1946.

Sinha, N. K. : Midnapur Salt Papers, Calcutta, 1954.

- Economic History of Bengal, 2 Vols, Calcutta, 1961-62.

Singh, Hiralal : Problems and policies of British in India, London, 1963.

Smith, R. B. : Life of Lord Lawrence, 2 Vols, London, 1883.

Spear, Percival : Oxford history of modern India, Oxford, 1965.

Stirling, A : Orissa - its geography, statistics and history.

: Religion and Antiquities, London, 1846.

: An account (geographical, statistical and historical) of Orissa proper or Cuttack, Calcutta, 1904.

Stocks, Eric : The English utilitarians and India, Oxford, 1959.

Strachey, Richard : The finances and public works of India from 1869 to 1881, London, 1882.

Strachey John : India-its administration and progress, 3rd edition, London, 1903.

Sudaram and Dutta : Indian Economy, New Delhi, 1989.

Sunderland, J. T : India in Bondage, Calcutta, 1928.

Taylor, William : Famines in India - their remedy and prevention, London, 1874. Thirtyeight years in India, Vol.I, London, 1881.

Temple, Richard : Men and event of my time in India, London, 1882.

Thomas P. J. : Mercantilism and East India Trade, London, 1963.

Thomson, Edward and Garrat, G. J. : Rise and fulfillment of British rule in India, London, 1934.

Tripathy, A. : Trade and finance in Bengal presidency, 1793-1833, Calcutta, 1956.

Tripathy, R. : Crafts and commerce in Orissa, Delhi, 1986, 1803-1828.

Toynbee, G. A. : A sketch of the history of Orissa, Calcutta, 1873.

Trevelyan, Charles : A report upon the Inland Customs and Town Duties of Bengal presidency, Calcutta, 1835.

Trotter, L. J., History of Indian under Queen Victoria, 2 Vols, London, 1886.

Vakil, C. N. and others : Growth of trade and industry in modern India, Calcutta, 1931.

Watt, Sir George : Commercial products of India, London, 1908.

: Dictionary of the economic products of India, Calcutta, 1823.

Wheeler, James Talboys and Macmillan, Michad

: European traveller in India, Calcutta, 1956.

Wheeler, W : Salt Manual of 1903, Calcutta, 1903.

Wilson, C. R. : The early annals of the English in Bengal, Vol. I and II, Calcutta, 1895.

Woodruff, Phillip : The Men who ruled India, Vol.II, London, 1954.

BOOKS (ORIYA)

Acharya P. M : Orissa Itihasa (Oriya), Cuttack, 1925.

Das S. N. : Unabinsa Satabdira Orissa, (Oriya), Part-I, Calcutta, 1969.

Das, S. P. : Sambalpur Itihas (Oriya), Sambalpur, 1962.

Mahatab, H. K. : Sadhanara Pathe (Oriya), Cuttack, 1972.

Mohanty, Surendra : Satabdira Surya (Oriya), Cuttack, 1920.

: Madhusudan Das (Oriya) Cuttack, 1972.

Mishra, Godavarish : Half a century of Orissa and my place in it (Oriya), Cuttack, 1972.

Pattanaik, Sudhakar : Sambada Patraru Odisara Katha (Oriya), Cuttack, 1972.

Rajguru, S. N. : Odisara Itihasa (Oriya), Vol. I, 1985.

Ray, B. C., Sahitya Sanskruti-O-Itihasa (Oriya), Bhubaneswar, 1990.

- Ardha Satabdira Odissa (Oriya), BBSR, 1996.

- Bilpabi Bira Jagabandhu (Oriya), BBSR, 1996.

Senapati, Fakir Mohan : Atmajevani Charita (Oriya), Reprint, Cuttack, 1969.

GLOSSARY

Abkari	Excise (Opium, Ganja and Liquor).
Abra	A superior variety of Kurkhutch salt.
Abwab	Miscellaneous casses, charges levied by Zamindars or Public officers illegally in addition to the regular assessment on the land.
Aurang	A manufacturing division of salt agency.
Baboo	Clerks engaged in revenue offices, especially Bengalis.
Bazar	A market.
Bepari	A businessman, a dealer, a merchant.
Bhowry	A house for boiling salt.
Chowkey	A station of police or of customs, a post where a guard is posted.
Chowkidar or Choukidar	A village watchman, a police or customs peon.
Churrus	A narcotic and intoxicant, a portion of hemp plant.
Dadni	Advance payment.
Darogah or Daroga	An officer-in-charge of the division

	of salt agency of a police station, a manager, a superintendent especially the chief native officer of police, customs or excise station.
Ganja	A kind of intoxicating drug prepared from the hemp plant, an intoxicant used by the people.
Garhjat	Tributary states of Orissa.
Gola	A warehouse, a place where grain or salt is kept for a season, also a grain or salt market, a place where grain or salt is sold wholesale.
Hat	A market held on certain days in a week.
Jamadar	An officer of police, customs or excise, second to the darogah.
Kahan	A measure of Kauri currency.
Kauri	A small shell found in Indian ocean used as money.
Koomtees	A merchantile community from Madras presidency.
Kothi	A store room.
Kurkutch or Karkatch	Salt obtained by solar evaporation.
Mahajan	A money-lender, banker, creditor.
Mahula or Mowah	A small fruit of a tree out of which liquor is prepared locally.
Malangi	A manufacturer of salt.
Mela	A seasonal fair.

Maund	Forty seers (one seer = 2.0532 lbs).
Padhan	A class of proprietory tenure holder.
Pana	A sum of 80 kaurishells equal to 20 gandas, 16 panas make a kahan.
Panga	Salt produced by boiling the brine.
Rawana	A pass, a certificate from a collector of customs authorising goods to pass without payment of further duty, a passport.
Sahukar	Indigenous banker and money-lender.
Sanad	A grant, a charter.
Sayer	Taxes other than land revenue, transit duties.
Sicca	A stamped coin, especially the name the silver currency of the Moghul kings adopted by the Indian princes and eventually by the East India Company.
Sirastadar	A record-keeper.
Taidad	A document of contract of salt manufacture.
Tari	Fermented juice of palm tree.
Zilla	A district, a division.

ABBREVIATIONS

AGAR	...	Annual General Administration Report
ARG	...	Abstract of Regulations of Government
BAR	...	Bengal Administrative Report
BCHR	...	Balasore Custom House Records
BDG	...	Bengal District Gazetteer
BJP	...	Bengal Judicial Proceedings
BRP	...	Bengal Revenue Proceedings
BRR	...	Board of Revenue (Orissa) Records
BSA	...	Bengal State Archieves
BSR	...	Balasore Salt Records
CPC	...	Calendar of Persian Correspondence
DSM	...	Diary of Streynsham Master
DWH	...	Diary of Willium Hedges
EFI	...	English Factories in India
GAROD	...	General Administration Report of Orissa Division
IGI	...	Imperial Gazetteer of India
IFC	...	Indian Famine Commission
IHRC	...	Indian Historical Record Commission
JBRS	...	Journal of Bihar, Orissa Research Society
JRAS	...	Journal of Royal Asiatic Society
Maddox Report	...	Final Report on the Survey and Settlement of the province of Orissa

		1890-1900 by S. L. Maddox
OHRJ	...	Orissa Historical Research Journal
OSA	...	Orissa State Archieves
PBCSO	...	Proceedings of Board of Customs, Salt and Opium
PBT	...	Proceedings of the Board of Trade
RAB	...	Report on the Administration of Bengal
RAC	...	Report of the Administration of Customs
RAR	...	Report on the Abkari Revenue
RBR	...	Records of the Board of Revenue.
RIF	...	Report on the Indian Famine Commission
Rundell's Report	...	Report on the manufacture of salt and the system of administration of salt Revenue of Balasore, Cuttack and Puri districts forming Orissa division of Bengal presidency
Secy.	...	Secretary
U. D.	...	Utkal Dipika

INDEX

L

M